The Elements Of Internet Style

search easy-access hierarchy wiki

media-agnostic e-readers browsers intranet handhelds

webinar webrary bioneering

high-touch interactive

blogosphere millennials literacies

The New Rules of Creating Valuable Content
for Today's Readers

THE EDITORS OF EEI PRESS

Library social networking chunking catablog sticky links FAQ

customizable cyberiffic future-proof RSS

ALLWORTH PRESS
NEW YORK

EEI PRESS
A Division of EEI Communications

The content of this book is © 2007 by EEI Press®, a division of EEI Communications, a publishing services, training, outsourcing, and advisory firm. Send requests for reprint permission to 66 Canal Center Plaza, Suite 200, Alexandria, VA 22314-5507 or send e-mail to press@eeicom.com. For more resources related to this book, including a blog, come to eeicom.com/press.

All rights in all media are reserved. No part of this book may be reproduced, repurposed, stored, or distributed in any form or in any medium without written permission. Send inquiries to press@eeicom.com.

Some material was adapted from articles that originally appeared in a different form in *The Editorial Eye* newsletter, published by EEI Press. Excerpts from NetLingo, the Internet Dictionary (netlingo.com) are © Erin Jansen and used with permission.

Copublished with Allworth Press, which has exclusive rights for sales to the trade. Allworth Press is an imprint of Allworth Communications, Inc., 10 East 23rd Street, New York, NY 10010. Send inquiries about terms and discounts to pub@allworth.com.

Cover design by Derek Bacchus
Interior design and typography by SR Desktop Services, Ridge, NY

ISBN-13: 978-1-58115-492-4
ISBN-10: 1-58115-492-5

Library of Congress Cataloging-in-Publication Data
    The elements of Internet style : the new rules of creating valuable content for today's readers / the editors of EEI Press.
        p.   cm.
    Rev. ed. of: E-what? Alexandria, VA : EEI Press, 2000.
    Includes index.
    ISBN-13: 978-1-58115-492-4 (pbk.)
    ISBN-10: 1-58115-492-5 (pbk.)
    1. Web sites—Design.   2. Authorship—Style manuals.   3. Internet publishing.
4. Digital media.   I. E-what?
TK5105.888E24   2007
006.7—dc22
                                                                              2007038461

Printed in the United States

Table of Contents

Preface: What New Rules?   **v**
*Actively learning, practicing openness to change, and conserving
only the most important standards are essential to communication
careers in the 21st century*

Acknowledgments   **ix**

Excerpt from the Foreword to the First Edition   **xi**

1   **The New Publishing Landscape and Lexicon**   **1**
*Many new-media buzzwords come packed in conceptual fuzziness
that makes it hard to keep up with, much less master, electronic
communication and publishing tools*

2   **Creating Valuable Content: The Internet Influence**   **11**
*We have to broaden our definition of audience and of literacy—
pluralizing both—but the thundering migration to myriad versions
of online content by no means makes all printed content obsolete
or even inferior*

3   **Connecting with Tomorrow's Readers, Customers,
and Colleagues**   **19**
*No psychographic profile can pinpoint the traits of all individuals.
But publishers would be foolish not to align their message strategies
with the preferences of the readers they most need to reach:
traditional-media-resistant millennials*

4   **Understanding What Web 2.0 Means for Editors and Writers**   **29**
*The new publishing mandate—inviting information users to
contribute to mediated content—requires editors and publishers
to see the value of genuine interactivity, and encourage it*

5   **Listening to People Talk: How Conversational Media Works**   **35**
*When it's lively, informational, responsive, and civilized, public
talk can build community, forge personal loyalty, and affect
corporate reputations*

6   Shaping Information for Its Users: The Pursuit of Usefulness   47
*When publishers go beyond organizing content the way they want
people to use it and allow different ways to access self-selected
information, users repay that increased relevance with
their attention*

7   Web Style: Writing, Organizing, Editing   55
*Web style integrates content and presentation in ways directly
pegged to the capabilities of online information search, navigation,
linking, and sharing—so good Web writing isn't just a plugged-in
version of writing for the page*

8   The Rules Used to Matter. What Now?   81
*We can't deny the energy that Internet publishing has brought to
traditional editorial gatekeeping, which has been characterized,
not to put too fine a point on it, as, uh, well, dead. But excellence
in written and graphic communications is still the goal*

9   You've Got a Style of Your Own   105
*Creating an organizational style guide (or style sheet) takes time
and effort, but once it exists, you'll wonder how you got along
without it*

10   New Usage: Adventuresome, Troublesome, or Tiresome?   125
*The one thing editors and designers can count on is the steady
evolution toward down style, a trend toward omitting optional
but unnecessary—and possibly intrusive—capitalization,
punctuation, and special emphasis. The less complexity, the better*

11   Coda: The Future of the Book   153
*"The new digital genres require rethinking and relearning the
craft of authorship, and there are still many stories best told through
the traditional linear book and many arguments best presented as
lengthy textual passages."—Clifford Lynch*

Appendix: Resources for Continuing Education   **167**

Index   **173**

Preface: What New Rules?

Every year, the Society for Scholarly Publishing brings together the players in the traditional scholarly publishing community—publishers, editors, librarians, scholars, printers, agents, wholesalers, booksellers, and others—to hear about new developments in such areas of concern to them as content licensing, copyright, business usage data, and academic publishing.

The program theme of the 2007 annual meeting: "Imagining the Future: Scholarly Communication 2.0." Featured speaker: Tim O'Reilly, who coined the phrase Web 2.0. The hot central question behind the sessions: "Is Web 2.0 just a buzzword, or are there real opportunities for scholarly publishing lying beneath the hype? Find out how evolving Internet strategies and technologies can empower you and your organization." Other presenters included Larry Sanger (Wikipedia/Citizendium), Paul Duguid (UC Berkeley), and David Worlock (Outsell, Inc.).

And this is the *traditional* publishing crowd. You're reading this book not a moment too soon.

Copublished with Allworth Press in New York, *Elements* is the revised version of the award-winning EEI Press book *E-What? A Guide to the Quirks of New Media Style and Usage.* We've partnered to offer insights about today's new readers and new publishing models, which can be hard to glean on the fly from many different sources.

Mainstream reliance on the Internet as a publishing medium has grown since the early 1990s to influence nearly every segment of society today: churches, small merchants, universities, hospitals, charities, museums, multinational corporations, and newspaper, magazine, and book publishers. Also local, state, and federal government agencies. Also teenagers, nutcases, politicos, pornographers, crooks, and your talented cousin Kathy, a pen-and-ink and watercolor artist.

All of these and more tell their stories, sell their wares, and make their cases on the Web. Thus, to understand what we mean by *The New Rules of Creating Valuable Content for Today's Readers* takes a working knowledge of core communication concepts and terms directly related to the influence of the Internet.

Some sound so deceptively familiar that you may still be taking them for granted. Some are so new that you may have been ignoring their new implications as irrelevant to your still-largely-print-based work up until now.

Whatever your particular spot on the new-media learning curve, you need to be aware of the implications of these terms, which have fundamentally altered as Internet use and portable publishing technologies have evolved: *literacy, community, user-generated content, conversational media, Web writing style. Information search, access, hierarchy, and usability. Standard American English usage. Editing. Publishing. Reading. Content.*

This book's focus is framed by a handful of essential rules—attitudes, really—that all who aspire to creating valuable content for their audiences will take to heart:

- Keep alive a relentless curiosity about effective ways to craft and present comprehensible, credible, useful messages.
- Show respect for the diverse needs and preferences of the wide world of information seekers by making informed structural decisions that allow multiple avenues of access.
- Strive for a flexible attitude toward linguistic informality and innovation without abandoning the imperatives of correct grammar, consistent style, accurate reporting, clear writing, and user-focused design.
- Stay aware of and open to research on usability, readability, and shifting demographics; and new publishing technologies.
- Accept the fact that readers want help not only finding what's relevant to them but also avoiding what's not. Today's information seekers hate wasting time. An honestly packaged communication agenda is a strategic asset even when it says to some people "not for you."

Perhaps most of all, work at staving off cynicism. Allow yourself to welcome (or at least keep a wary eye out for) each announcement of the Next Cool Thing coming out of the yearly International Consumer Electronics Show. Accept with as much grace as possible the truth that being a content creator means a life of instability: learning, relearning, unlearning.

Everyday, we make leaps of faith in the power of written and visual communications. We can't do that if, like Road Runner crossing a canyon on a high wire, we look down and let all the electronica we don't own, don't know how to use, and haven't even heard of intimidate us.

Half of this edition is entirely new and half is extensively updated. All of it offers guidance for setting a consistent, contemporary editorial style that will serve you well in print and online. You may not agree with everything in the newly added analyses of pivotal trends, but you cannot afford to ignore them—or the influence of the Internet on print publishing.

The chapter on Web style goes beyond "write it short, chunk it, and link it" to offer perspective on readying publications for more than one destination. Chapters on maintaining distinctions that still matter and handling new usage encourage you to make decisions that aid readers, regardless of the publishing medium. Letting go of overly complex, counterproductive, outdated rules, and rules that were never truly rules at all, is a part of the editorial decisionmaking process.

The chapter on compiling proprietary style guides encourages you to follow intelligent precedents and trust yourself to make your own exceptions. Those responsible for making proprietary style decisions when the traditional authorities are silent or disagree are contributing to the new Standard American English lexicon—so we recommend being able to explain the rationale for nonstandard style and usage, beyond "we've always done it that way" and "nobody remembers why we do it that way."

We end with an only slightly ironic coda on the future of book publishing. It's a negotiated settlement between the comfort of static printed content and the undeniable pragmatic pull of e-content. An appendix of useful resources for continuing education follows, and an index to aid quick lookup. But quite honestly, this book is meant to be read thoughtfully, critically—not hit-and-run.

And to that end, in this book, we've chosen to honor legitimate style alternatives in directly quoted excerpts, as well as other proprietary style preferences, even when they differ from EEI Press and Allworth Press style. So in a quotation that uses British English style, we do not alter that convention of placing a comma outside the ending quotation mark. And if one company does not use a comma before *Inc.* in its name, we do not insert it, but if another company does, we retain the comma. This means that skimming readers might think they're superficial inconsistencies. Well, they are—but it's deliberate. In a book about the influence of the Internet, this seems apt. Web users encounter various Englishes, even on the same site, if the content comes from authors who have US, Canadian, British, and other kinds of native English.

In general, targeted-information seekers are less interested in utterly consistent mechanical style than editors believe, as long as treatments are nonintrusive and as consistent as possible within a given micro-context. Waffling and decisionmaking nonstandard in any widely used style, in the same document or across a series of closely linked items, are what rattles reader confidence in a publisher's professionalism and the value of content.

An integral element of Internet style—of all forms of publishing, really—is us. Idiosyncratic, emotional, one-of-a-kind human beings, we're still interested in the sound of the human voice, the extension of a helping hand. More than ever, in the Age of Information Sharing, we are in the game of clear communications together. We're grateful whenever a message seems meant for us.

The medium may be the message du jour, but publishing ultimately devolves upon labor-intensive investments of time, attention, care, trust, wit, technical skill, judgment, common sense, and—so we like to think—goodwill. We still seem to have an awful lot to say to one another, don't we? Stop by eeicom.com/press/istyle to continue the conversation.

Linda Jorgensen, for the Editors of EEI Press
Spring 2007

Acknowledgments

In keeping with the trend toward collaborative publishing projects, this book was copublished with Allworth Press and updated by EEI Press editors with the help of knowledgeable contributors who are also excellent writers. We thank them for their distinctive voices and perspectives.

MERRY BRUNS (Washington, DC), a nationally recognized content strategist, and Web writing and editing trainer since 1994, wrote about Web style and taking printed content online. Founder of ScienceSites Communications, she has been a consultant for BBC London, Porter-Novelli, the Centers for Disease Control, Harvard Medical School, the US Environmental Protection Agency, Accenture, the National Academy of Sciences, NASA/Goddard, Georgetown University, and the World Bank. Her Web site is sciencesitescom.com.

JESSICA DEGRAFFENREID (Memphis, TN) wrote about the expectations and preferences of the demographic called the millennials—tomorrow's readers and communicators. A communications and media specialist, she is director of communications for Chi Omega, the world's largest women's fraternal organization. She has been a political communication strategist in the telecommunications, aerospace, global health, and environmental sectors.

MARY FUMENTO (Washington, DC) wrote about the future of the printed book and the impact of e-books on libraries, booksellers, writers, and booklovers. A librarian and Web developer, she specializes in electronic document management with an emphasis on Web technology. She is past president of DC Web Women and the founder of Webcaplib.org, a nonprofit professional organization that connects libraries with the digital world and educates them about new media.

AMY GAHRAN (Boulder, CO) the creator of the popular Web site Contentious, wrote about conversational media and how to mediate vital online communities. As a consultant, content strategist, and freelance writer-editor, she helps organizations and professionals raise a clear, strong voice in the public conversation, especially through resourceful use of online media. Her Web site is rightconversation.com.

ROY JACOBSEN (Fargo, ND) wrote about shaping information for maximum usefulness to its users. A part-time technical writer and freelance writer-editor, he has been writing and editing for more than 20 years in a variety of fields, most recently software development, and is a contributing editor for *The Editorial Eye*. His Web site is rmjacobsen.squarespace.com.

LEE MICKLE (Alexandria, VA), an EEI Communications editor, coauthored much of the first edition (with Kathryn Hall) and helped update the new chapter on setting standards with proprietary style guidelines. She has written inhouse style guides for EEI clients and was an editor of *The Copyeditor's Guide to Substance and Style: Learn How to Find and Fix Errors in Text and Graphics, in Print and Online* (EEI Press).

JANET MULLANY (Alexandria, VA) researched and wrote about the Eyetrack study of online reading patterns and the implications of the Internet for global literacy. An EEI Communications proofreader and bookseller, and assistant editor of *The Editorial Eye*, she has worked as an archaeologist, a classical-music radio announcer, and a performing-arts publicist. She writes historical women's fiction for HarperCollins. Her Web site is janetmullany.com.

TAYLOR WALSH (Silver Spring, MD) wrote about Web 2.0, predicting that mediation (editing) will continue to play an important role in user-generated online content. The publisher of Lifepages.net, a healthcare media company, he has been a leading developer of innovative Web content and social networking services since the 1980s, and a journalist, writer, and editor in the United States and abroad. His Web site is taylorw.wordpress.com.

From EEI Press, Linda Jorgensen was project editor; Robin Cormier and Mary Fumento reviewed the manuscript; Lee Mickle, Judy Cleary, and Courtney Cox checked it; and Lee Ann Ragan indexed it.

From Allworth Press, headed by Tad Crawford, Derek Bacchus designed the cover; Susan Ramundo produced the layout; and Nicole Potter-Talling and Allison Caplin reviewed the manuscript.

Excerpt from the Foreword to the First Edition

The Internet would be easy to understand and talk and write about if only it would stop changing every week—but instead, some novel terms of art turn into hackneyed clichés and others become mainstream shorthand.

I started writing about the online world for the *Washington Post* in mid-1994; in a lot of ways, I'm still figuring out what is and is not obvious about all this. The linguistic target keeps moving, and I don't expect this situation to change for a long time. The point of the text we're working on shouldn't keep moving around, however, and that's why a guidebook like this is helpful. In self-defense, as we try to keep up with the fluidity of Internet style, we need some baselines.

Here's a baseline we can all agree on: Writing and speaking about the Web, and about any other technical topic—quantum physics, the history of NASA's Apollo program, automotive maintenance, or Bruce Springsteen bootlegs—should aim to nail down meanings without clouting the thumb of the everyday reader. Unnecessary jargon, unexplained acronyms, and jarring inconsistencies can quash attention and slow comprehension.

Consider, for instance, the issue of how to describe Usenet newsgroups—a topic that, about a decade ago, provoked constant arguments on the alt.internet.media-coverage newsgroup (itself a casualty of Internet evolution—here today, gone today).

Coverage in the mass media would most often describe these forums as *Internet message boards* or *online bulletin boards*. The true believers, who had been holding forth on Usenet for years before any newspaper had an inkling that a story could originate there, flamed (that is, vituperatively criticized) the "old media" for "not getting it." Meanwhile, the few journalists online at that point argued, essentially, "Look, nobody's going to be that confused by this term, and at least people will have a chance of getting the analogy."

Those journalists had a point, but they were wrong. Not referring to Usenet as Usenet or newsgroups as newsgroups meant that readers had no easy way of trying this resource out for themselves with their own software, which didn't and still doesn't use terms like *message boards* or *bulletin boards*. Details do matter—especially since readers can go check things out for themselves.

A similar debate has been going on about how to specify a Web site's location (which, incidentally, I don't call a *URL* unless I'm writing for a technical audience—what's wrong with "address"?). If you simply specify the domain name, you can save a lot of trouble all around. One, plenty of Web-based companies include the *.com* extension in their names, so the name *is* the Web address. Two, almost all current Web browsers will fill in the *www.* and *http://* prefixes for you—why make the reader type in extra characters?

But on the other hand, there's no shortage of Web addresses that *don't* start with *www.*—not to mention the few heretical Web addresses that depart from the standard *http://*. (For instance, banking and other sites may start with *https://*, with that *s* denoting an encrypted connection secured against eavesdropping.)

Hence, I continue to insist on the full Web address. I am losing this fight, though, both at my office and in this book. It grates on me—why not be consistent and minimize reader confusion?—but I have, so far, been unable to drag everybody else along. (People become quite passionate about these matters. We editors take pride in the inventive patches we've used to construct our preferred-usage crazy quilts.)

I do have one consolation, though: The fashion for addresses, along with other Internet-related conventions, will almost certainly change yet again. But we're not going to make deadlines, and we're not going to be taken seriously, if we start from scratch stylistically every day. We can't wait until matters of style settle down; we have work to do today.

This book can help you settle an argument or start one, if you need to, perhaps with the guy down the hall who insists on lowercasing the *web* but wants you to know that he is a *Webmaster*. Editors are still the arbiters of much that is happening in publishing; they have their work cut out for them. Fortunately, they have this book.

Rob Pegoraro (rob@twp.com)
Consumer electronics editor, *Washington Post*
Spring 2000

1

The New Publishing Landscape and Lexicon

Remember those classic TV commercials with the lonely Maytag repairman? He gamely waited for service calls from customers whose appliances never needed fixing. The character actor who played him for many years died, and Maytag vice president Jeff Davidoff told *Parade* magazine (March 12, 2007) what the manufacturer was seeking in his replacement: "We want to revamp that 40-year-old TV character. We're in search of a new spokesman who is more edgy and hip."

Edginess—even bleeding-edginess—and a hip attitude (whatever that means—mainstream hipness is always a few steps behind the truly avant-garde) are part of the zeitgeist. But a "more edgy and hip" appliance spokesperson?

Trying too hard to *seem* edgy can backfire. Take, for example, a beat-up, windowless van spewing exhaust fumes and driven by a tired-looking guy in a ballcap and jumpsuit. The van sported a neatly lettered sign: "Pest Control for the 21st Century!" The boast seems weird—are the bugs of the millennium different, or the poisons?

But aside from that sort of posing, the cultural and intellectual spirit of the times is anchored in one all-encompassing attribute: newness. Wave after wave of newness. New thinking, redefined roles. Redefined standards, new vocabulary, redefined mandates. And almost all the newness is based on unprecedented communication and publishing capabilities. New is the new normal.

Innovation itself—the process of making new things and remaking old things—can be a threat, a promise, a boon, and a stressor. We're too close to the zeitgeist to see it clearly; it's all happening so fast, and the ripple effects are so far-reaching.

Not everyone is enthusiastic about being bombarded 24/7 by a relentless flow of gadgets, new versions of software, and streams of data. A strong undercurrent of nostalgia for low-tech creature comforts and high-touch business encounters pulls counter to the sea-change default. What do many people use their huge flatscreen wall TVs for during winter holiday parties? The image of a roaring fire in a homey brick fireplace, with centuries-old music wafting from digital speakers.

As many familiar toys, tools, and touchstones are replaced by "improved" versions, a feeling of confidence in our mastery of the basics is another casualty. Despite decades of respectable print-world chops, some pros feel they're losing traction. Newcomers to the content-creation game can become impatient with the angst of their elders: "What's the big deal? You taught us in school that change is the only constant, so why get upset about constant change?"

Regardless of how instantly, frequently, or cheerfully we adopt the Next Big Thing, all of us have homework to do. The future belongs to those who find the way forward without forgetting that the point of publishing is to meet the needs of our audiences. New technology does not change that— though it has altered the traditional relationships between content creator, publisher, and audience.

So we begin with a handful of words that are inextricable from the new landscape—a word we use wryly, since *land* has little to do with it (Netscape was taken). Simply following the synonyms and examples leads to greater awareness of the concepts driving the Internet age. What exactly does *electronic* mean, anyway? What's the difference between *new media* and *multimedia*? *Digital* and *electronic* and *wireless*? *The Internet* and *the Web*?

Precision and clarity in personal and professional writing matter more than ever, not less, as we all struggle to find relevant, meaningful information in a virtual whiteout of talk and data. Making a typo is not the worst thing in the world; wasting the time of people honoring you with their attention is.

A caveat: Even the broad range of technical sources cited in these definitions do not agree completely on what exactly each term means. But that doesn't mean conserving clear usage distinctions is obsolete. It's proof that assuming "they'll know what I'm saying—keep it loose, it's the Internet" is risky. A speedily, globally relayed message that misses its mark is just a handbasket to hell on wheels.

Chew on these terms; let them lead you to others; keep asking questions. This Internet thing isn't a done deal, you know. We're making it up as we go, which means we have a say in the directions it takes.

new media. The term *new media* is most often used now to refer to all nonprinted media. But it gets tossed around.

From *webopedia.com:*

A generic term for the many different forms of electronic communication that are made possible through the use of computer technology. The term is in relation to "old" media forms, such as print newspapers and magazines, that are static representations of text and graphics. New media includes:

- Web sites
- streaming audio and video
- chat rooms
- e-mail
- online communities
- Web advertising
- DVD and CD-ROM media
- virtual reality environments
- integration of digital data with the telephone, such as Internet telephony
- digital cameras
- mobile computing

Use of the term *new media* implies that the data communication is happening between desktop and laptop computers and handhelds, such as PDAs, and the media they take data from, such as compact discs and floppy disks.

Uh oh. That definition, updated in August 2003, already seems old. It's missing some significant media forms: blogs, RSS, and instant messaging, for starters. Know anyone who's sent data via cell phone from a floppy disk lately? This just goes to show that even Web resources have trouble keeping up with the times.

multimedia. This definition from wikipedia.com illustrates how easy it is to follow Web links to related terms, growing your tech vocabulary and gaining a conceptual foundation:

Uses multiple forms of information content and information processing (e.g., text, audio, graphics, animation, video, interactivity) to inform or entertain the (user) audience. *Multimedia* also refers to the use of (but is not limited to) electronic media to store and experience multimedia content. Multimedia is similar to traditional mixed media in fine art, but with a broader scope. The term "rich media" is synonymous with interactive multimedia.

From answers.com:
Of or relating to the combined use of several media: a multimedia installation at the art gallery.

From scala.com:
The term multimedia describes a number of diverse technologies that allow visual and audio media to be combined in new ways for the purpose of

communicating. Applications include entertainment, education and advertising. Multimedia often refers to computer technologies. Nearly every PC built today is capable of multimedia because they include a CD-ROM or DVD drive, and a good sound and video card (often built into the motherboard). But the term multimedia also describes a number of dedicated media appliances, such as digital video recorders (DVRs), interactive television, MP3 players, advanced wireless devices and public video displays.

Here's a grassroots example of multimedia (from a press release, edited): "The lyrics and music to the song 'I Sure Wish a Man Could Be More Like a Dog' were written by Gini Graham Scott, an Oakland book author and songwriter whose fascination with dogs led to a series of Web sites, books, and games about dogs such as doyoulooklikeyourdog.com and whatkindofdogareyou.com. There will be game videos soon, too"—and no doubt a song video.

digital. This is one of the most loosely used terms—and it has meanings outside computing, too. The definition from *PC Magazine*'s Web encyclopedia is the simplest and most accurate:

> Traditionally, digital means the use of numbers and the term comes from digit, or finger. Today, digital is synonymous with computer. See also Digital Equipment.

More from pcmag.com/encyclopedia:

The 0s and 1s of digital data mean more than just on and off. They mean perfect copying. When information, music, voice and video are turned into binary digital form, they can be electronically manipulated, preserved and regenerated perfectly at high speed. The millionth copy of a computer file is exactly the same as the original. While this continually drives the software and content publishers crazy protecting their copyrights, it is nevertheless a major advantage of digital processing.

From neoninc.com:
Describes a method of storing, processing and transmitting information through the use of distinct electronic or optical pulses that represent the binary digits 0 and 1. Digital transmission/switching technologies employ a sequence of discrete, distinct pulses to represent information, as opposed to the continuously variable analog signal.

From thefreedictionary.com:
Computer science: Of or relating to a device that can read, write, or store information that is represented in numerical form. See Usage Note at virtual.

Electronics: The branch of physics that deals with the emission and effects of electrons and with the use of electronic devices. A circuit or device that represents magnitudes in digits: digital computer. Using or giving a reading in digits: digital clock. Displaying numbers rather than scale positions: digital clock, digital readout.

wireless. From searchnetworking.techtarget.com, just a few of a slew of definitions from other Web sites—all slightly different:

- Using the radio-frequency spectrum for transmitting and receiving voice, data and video signals for communications. (braddye.com/glossary.html)
- Refers to communications, monitoring or control systems in which electromagnetic or acoustic waves carry a signal through atmospheric space rather than along a wire. (voiceanddata.com.au/vd/admin/glossary.asp)
- Refers to the type of broadband connection where information is sent from and arrives at a computer through transmission towers. (largebande.gc.ca/pub/technologies/bbdictionary.html)
- Refers to telecommunication in which electromagnetic waves (rather than some form of wire) carry the signal over part or all of the communication path. Some monitoring devices, such as intrusion alarms, employ acoustic waves at frequencies above the range of human hearing; these are also sometimes classified as wireless. (grb.uk.com/263.0.html)
- A general designation for communication without wires. In networking, common wireless standards include 802.11b and Bluetooth. Both standards broadcast over the 2.4 gigahertz band. Cellular, satellite, microwave, and infrared broadcasting are also forms of wireless communication. (atmmarketplace.com/news_story_10150.htm)
- The ability of a computer to access e-mails and the Internet without being physically connected by cable. (winters.co.uk/factsheets/ecommerce.html)
- The nodes or computers on a wireless LAN do not hook up to each other with wires, but communicate with microwave or infrared transmission. (sqatester.com/glossary/)
- Network or device using electromagnetic waves—including rf, infrared, laser, visible light and acoustic energy—for transmissions. (sb-systems.com/mobile-phones-glossary-window.html)
- Wireless was an old-fashioned term for a radio receiver, referring to its use as a wireless telegraph. The term is widely used to describe modern wireless connections such as wireless broadband Internet. (en.wikipedia.org/wiki/Wireless)

As an illustration of how hard it can be to pin down tech terms with overlapping applications, this definition-by-example from proxicast.com/support/glossary.htm requires us to understand what wireless is by recognizing terms for what it does: "Without wires, or any telecommunication that uses broadcast (radio) technology versus copper wires (land lines). Most typically, cellular or digital communications."

The last word is a contrarian definition of *wireless* from a cable manufacturer, bwcecom.belden.com/college/Cable101/wire%20glossary.htm:

> Really a misnomer. Belden makes a variety of cables needed to build the transmitting infrastructure required to support "wireless" devices. Wireless is a technology that allows a device (phone, pager or satellite dish) to be unconnected from the transmission point of a voice, video or data signal. The transmission infrastructure required to support such wireless devices is a wired platform of transmission towers and stations that communicate point to point and to telephone central offices.

Internet. We say this is a book about Internet style; let us now admit that we are using the term *Internet* loosely to mean all the ways and means that allow digitally powered collaborative, decentralized, and customized publishing. And by *publishing* we mean both (a) the act or process of preparing written and graphic material for presentation to an audience and (b) putting information into the public arena. Note that by written we don't mean only printed; Internet content is built one word or image at a time, just like printed content.

Here's a more contemporary definition from paperwise.com: "Publishing is the routing of content to the appropriate recipients either through paper or electronically through portals, an intranet, an extranet, email, or fax." (An extranet is a public Web site.)

Along with many professional publishers, when we say *Internet style* we're talking not about the technology per se but about what it allows communicators to do: reach audiences one at a time, or via niche or broad-spectrum public sites and forums. Broad- and narrowcast the same content in different presentations to localized, regional, and international audiences. Bring people together in communities and on sites that allow them to sample possibilities and select for themselves what's useful enough to take in and take away.

But in the interest of precision, we acknowledge that *the Internet* is not a synonym for everything electronic. It's not a synonym for *the Web*, either.

As webopedia.com distinguishes them: "The Internet, not the Web, is used for e-mail, which relies on SMTP, Usenet news groups, instant messaging, and FTP. The Web is just a portion of the Internet, albeit a large portion, and the two terms are not synonymous and should not be confused." More on the Internet from webopedia:

> A global network connecting millions of computers. More than 100 countries are linked into exchanges of data, news and opinions.
>
> Unlike online services, which are centrally controlled, the Internet is decentralized by design. Each Internet computer, called a *host*, is independent. Its operators can choose which Internet services to use and which local services to make available to the global Internet community. Remarkably, this anarchy by design works exceedingly well. There are a variety of ways to access the Internet. Most online services...offer access to some Internet services. It is also possible to gain access through a commercial Internet Service Provider (ISP).

Finally, from a unanimous Federal Networking Council (FNC) Resolution, which was developed in consultation with the leadership of the Internet and Intellectual Property Rights (IPR) Communities, passed in October 1995:

> "Internet" refers to the global information system that—
> (i)   is logically linked together by a globally unique address space based on the Internet Protocol (IP) or its subsequent extensions/follow-ons;
> (ii) is able to support communications using the Transmission Control Protocol/Internet Protocol (TCP/IP) suite or its subsequent extensions/ follow-ons, and/or other IP-compatible protocols; and
> (iii) provides, uses or makes accessible, either publicly or privately, high-level services layered on the communications and related infrastructure described herein.

Web. It sounds old-fashioned to use *World Wide Web*; most of us have shortened it to *Web* by now. And most of us who are not Web historians or IT professionals conflate its meaning with *the Internet*.

> ### From webopedia.com's definition of World Wide Web:
> A system of Internet servers that support specially formatted documents. The documents are formatted in a markup language called HTML (HyperText Markup Language) that supports links to other documents, as well as graphics, audio, and video files. This means you can jump from one document to another simply by clicking on hot spots. Not all Internet servers are part of the World Wide Web.

There are several applications called Web browsers that make it easy to access the World Wide Web; two of the most popular [are] Netscape Navigator and Microsoft's Internet Explorer.

From Oracle's online glossary, orafaq.com:
An electronic network of computers that includes nearly every university, government, and research facility in the world. Also included are many commercial sites. It started with four interconnected computers in 1969 and was known as ARPANET.

Webopedia helpfully explains the basic difference between the Internet and the Web [edited]:

The *Internet* is a networking infrastructure that allows any computer to communicate with any other computer if both are connected to the Internet. Information that travels over the Internet does so via a variety of languages known as *protocols*; thus, the Internet infrastructure functions as a medium.

The *Web* is an information-sharing model built on top of the Internet—and it's just one of the ways information can be accessed from and disseminated over the Internet.

The Web uses the HTTP protocol to transmit data—and that's only one of the languages spoken over the Internet. Web services use HTTP to allow applications to exchange information. The Web also utilizes browsers to access Web documents, called Web pages, linked to each other via hyperlinks. Web documents can contain graphics, sounds, text, and video.

Web 2.0. In chapter 4, Taylor Walsh talks about the relevance of Web 2.0 for writers and editors. O'Reilly Media coined the phrase back in the old days of 2004 to refer to the so-called second generation of Web-based services—social networking sites, wikis, e-communication tools, and folksonomies—that emphasize online collaboration and sharing among users. *Folksonomy*, a term coined in 2004 by information architect Thomas Vander Wal, is, he says, the "personal free tagging of information and objects (anything with a URL) for one's own retrieval. The tagging is done in a social environment (shared and open to others). The act of tagging is done by the person consuming the information." An example is the photo-sharing Web site Flickr. (See what we mean about learning the vocabulary itself to shine a light on the new publishing models?)

In 2005, at the first Web 2.0 conference, Tim O'Reilly gave examples of companies or products that could exist only on the Internet, "deriving their power from the human connections and network effects Web 2.0 makes possible, and growing in effectiveness the more people use them." He named eBay, craigslist, Wikipedia, del.icio.us, Skype, dodgeball, and Adsense. A number of newer ones like digg.com would qualify, too.

O'Reilly provided a compact definition of Web 2.0 in 2006:

> Web 2.0 is the business revolution in the computer industry caused by the move to the Internet as platform, and an attempt to understand the rules for success on that new platform. Chief among those rules is this: Build applications that harness network effects to get better the more people use them.

The "Time bar of Web 2.0 buzz words," a graphic showing the evolution of Web 2.0 lingo, is worth looking for on webopedia.com.

The Internet isn't a magic medium, but it does have a powerful draw for people in search of information. That's how the Internet and the Web are justifying the continued existence and expansion of brick-and-mortar libraries, as well as bookstores (though stores online are faring better than stores on land).

The publishing landscape doesn't look the same, and the way we talk about it doesn't sound the same. Let's pack up the squirrelly technical lexicon for now and look at some factors influencing the creation of valuable content.

2

Creating Valuable Content:
The Internet Influence

Fears about new technology shaping and influencing society for the worst are nothing new. Consider this passage from Plato's Phaedrus, in which Socrates describes the creation of writing in Egyptian theology. A minor god, Theuth, presented this new tool to the god of all Egypt, Thamus, saying, "This will make the Egyptians wiser and give them better memories; it is a specific both for the memory and for the wit."

But when Thamus reviewed Theuth's other innovations (including mathematics, astronomy, and dice), he balked at the use of letters, saying, "This discovery of yours will create forgetfulness in the learners' souls, because they will not use their memories; they will trust to the external written characters and not remember of themselves."

In other words, people dependent on this daring innovation writing would inherently be less aware, less thoughtful, less capable. At the very least, that would disrupt the rhythms of society. Sounds familiar, doesn't it?

SOURCE OF OR CURE FOR LITERACY WOES?

We've become quite casual about the mainstreaming of the Web—we can't get through a nightly TV news show or morning classical radio program without being told there's more on a story or a playlist available on the station's Web site. Pointers in printed marketing, collateral, newsletters, magazines, journals, and books—including this one!—to visit Web sites for more and updated information are ubiquitous.

Will the drive toward digital and Web publishing and communications result in changes even more profound than now seems likely, eroding levels of literacy, standards of scholarship, and the viability of professional journalism?

Should print publishers scurry to placate the "lost" audience they envision flocking to spend time and money on the Web? Is it even possible or necessary to make all potential information seekers happy all the time?

Will those rushing their publishing programs online wind up, along with the artist's rep from Decca Records who turned the Beatles down, squirming in the special circle of hell reserved for embarrassed executives?

Will people, tired of being pushed to maintain a state of always-on, retreat from their arsenals of electronica and trade in their quick-and-dirty user behaviors for more thoughtful, civilized, "high-touch" business and interpersonal transactions?

There was a rash of speculative writing in the 1990s about the possibilities of the Web, defined by Stevan Harnad as the "fourth revolution" in human communication; the others are language, writing, and the printing press. Yet a decade later, the very issue of literacy, particularly in the developing world, is still pressing.

With the provision of universal primary education as one of the [Millennium] Development Goals, UNESCO estimates that 771 million people in the world, two-thirds of whom are women, are illiterate: "This is— for a fifth of the world's adult population—a serious violation of human rights. It also constitutes a major impediment to the realization of human capabilities and the achievement of equity and of economic and social development, particularly for women."

The National Institute for Literacy (nifl.gov) tells us that "The Workforce Investment Act of 1998 and the National Literacy Act of 1991 define literacy as 'an individual's ability to read, write, speak in English, compute and solve problems at levels of proficiency necessary to function on the job, in the family of the individual and in society.' This is a broader view of literacy than just an individual's ability to read, the more traditional concept of literacy."

Should we pat ourselves on the back, or hang our heads in shame, that in 1999 the Household Education Survey found that 50.2 percent of the US population aged over twenty-five had read a newspaper at least once a week, read one or more magazines regularly, and read one book in the past six months?

It may be too early to tell whether computers and the Web, at least in developed nations and the US in particular, are the source of or cure for literacy woes. What is evident to anyone who has the misfortune to read extensively online is that reading printed material is a vastly superior exercise with regard to ergonomics. However sophisticated a screen you use, pixilation of the font creates eyestrain and the upright position of the material, at arms length and eye level, is not comfortable.

ONLINE READABILITY ISSUES

Michael L. Bernard's study at the Software Usability Lab at Wichita State University shows that a 14-point, serif font lends itself to thorough reading. Steve Outing, in his report on the 2004 Eyetrack III study (more on this below) observes, "Smaller type encourages focused viewing behavior (that is, reading the words), while larger type promotes scanning. In general, our testing found that people spent more time focused on small type than large type. Larger type resulted in more scanning of the page—fewer words overall were fixated on—as people looked around for words or phrases that captured their attention."

But, wait—what exactly is a 14-point font on your computer screen? Your browser will allow you to change the font size, implying that if, for instance, you change it to a larger size, your concentration will go out the window, which is patently ridiculous.

The 1990s, when educators first began to speculate about the implications of the Internet, spawned much debate over the future of literacy. What's surprising is that the debate didn't continue. According to Charles A. Hill, activity dropped as participants realized their speculations were not fulfilled by developing technology. One "given" for the theorists of the 1990s, particularly those in English departments, was that there would be a lot more writing and more reading by students—and that texts online would become interactive, rather in the way video games have developed. Another universal prediction was that phones would become obsolete; no one foresaw the equally prevalent use of cell phones and e-mail, and the interaction between the two media.

Instead, Hill, writing in 1996, regretted the "disappearance of textual boundaries" in these terms: "Texts scroll on and off our screen, and we know that we are always looking at a small part of a work of indeterminable size."

Online amendments and editing by the author make the size and scope of a piece even more changeable. Further, hyperlinks and the decision of each reader to take them or not means that to a certain extent the reader, not the writer, determines the structure of a piece. Some online publications, notably Wikipedia, which thrives on reader amendment, further blur the distinctions between writer, reader, and editor.

Now, with both print and digital devices sharing the market, users may be frustrated by the limitations of print, but they are equally frustrated at being tethered to a desktop or laptop. The current generation of students, Hill comments, is better at multitasking—we all know teenagers who IM, talk on their cells, watch television, and do homework simultaneously. Has the ever-surprising human brain developed a filter system to deal with so much information from so many sources? Or, is this generation's approach merely superficial? In another decade we may have answers, or, more likely, further questions.

TRACKING WHAT THE EYE TRACKS

Another issue with reading material online is the way the eye behaves while viewing a computer screen. The established pattern of the eye on scanning a printed page—something Wall Street has known, and capitalized on, for decades—is, as you'd expect, a basic left to right pattern, reading from the beginning of one line to the end and then hopping diagonally backward to the beginning of the next, and so on in a series of zigzags. Faced with a page that is a blend of graphics and colors, the eye strives to make sense by imposing the familiar "Z" pattern, this time on the whole page.

Onscreen, it's a different story. The Poynter Organization's most recent eyetrack test, Eyetrack III (2004), examined how people read mock online news sites. The Z is still there—sort of—as the eye wanders around. The main difference is that instead of ending up safely in the lower right-hand corner (where, if this were an advertisement, a starburst would announce the final hard sell—fifty percent off today only!) the eye returns to the top of the screen. Here's a simplified version of this pattern, with the circle representing the starting point. In Eyetrack lingo, the angles are points of eye fixation, and the lines between them, saccades (amaze your friends at Scrabble!):

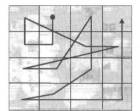

(This Eyetrack diagram appeared in an article by Steve Outing, "What News Websites Look Like Through Readers' Eyes," and is reprinted by permission of the Poynter Institute for Media Studies. See poynteronline.org for more on the Poynter-cosponsored Eyetrack studies.)

So the eye attempts to synthesize information in a different way, drawn in the last stage upward to the top of the screen—and this is a journey that takes fractions of a second. Owners of commercial Web sites know that, based on the first page they come to, consumers make the decision whether to stay on that site or not; and if they stay, what they will buy and whether they will return.

To return to the somewhat redundant information that a serif font leads to greater legibility—one of the standard conventions of typesetting—this is all to the good if the reader decides to print out material. For all the assertions of the last decade—Hill's ironic definition of the "late age of print" and Harnad's "post-Gutenberg galaxy"—printed material is still, for many circumstances, the best option. Of course, when an affordable e-reader is on the market, that too may change.

ERODING TEXTUAL BOUNDARIES

With the availability of so much information online—where, incidentally, most of the research for this chapter was done, using browser bookmarks and printouts studded with colored Post-its—how, if at all, has this changed reading and our approach to books? And what about students in high schools and colleges for whom the family computer was friend, companion, and babysitter? Are they frustrated with print material, used to getting the information now—now!—fractious and uncomfortable without the comforting glow of a monitor?

Not so, according to Dr. Leigh Ryan, director of the Writing Center at the University of Maryland College Park. She admits that students are far more comfortable online, and reading online, than older generations—ah, those young eyes. It makes you speculate that some dormant part of the human brain has fortuitously sprung into action, rather as you wonder exactly how the Exner's Writing Area in the left frontal lobe entertained itself during millennia of rock-banging. Visual rhetoric, according to Dr. Ryan, has replaced rhetoric as a subject, meaning that students' assignments are now expected to be multimedia, words enhanced by images.

The truth is, books are books, computers are computers, and we have different expectations for both. As for the much-vaunted hyperlinks and their perceived advantage, it is always the reader's choice to use them and it is the writer's responsibility to maintain the linear flow of his or her material. It's not possible to second-guess which links in a text will be clicked, but it is sensible to assume that a reader would like to see a figure, illustration, or other non-text feature near the text where it is mentioned.

Hill's concept of eroding textual boundaries raises some interesting possibilities for the print publisher. No, we're not suggesting that every book should become a Wikipedia, but discussion and further findings—particularly for a book like this where new information and stories come to light daily—can be continued on the Web, via a blog or forum.

As an example of new findings, here's an interesting twist to the digital vs. print issue—about readers becoming listeners. Associated Press reported that college-level students are using MP3 players to listen to downloaded material, and a year ago Apple launched iTunes U, where teachers can post lectures for students to download. Professor Kathy O'Connor at Tidewater College, with four campuses in Virginia got an $11,000 grant to provide students with iPods; other schools' libraries lend iPods to students. McGraw-Hill Cos., the leading textbook publisher, offers more than 800 digital products, an increase of 50 percent over the past 4 years. Leading digital book seller Audible, Inc. and Pearson Education joined forces in 2006 to launch VangoNotes, textbook chapter summaries and reviews in MP3 form.

Grade schools are also going digital, with Playaway—a two-ounce flash-player preloaded with an audio book made by Follett Corp. and Findaway World—which has been sold to school districts for about six months. On loan at over 1,000 libraries, 15 percent of which are school libraries, the players are seen as an adjunct to parents reading to their children, a practice long encouraged by educators to improve literacy and a love of books.

ARE WE REVERTING TO A PRE-LITERATE CULTURE?

Of course, it could be argued that increasing reliance on iPods and digital listening devices erodes our full potential as readers—that we're reverting to a pre-second-revolution stage (by Harnad's definition, we have speech but not writing). But a technical concept seems appropriate and reassuring in the context of the fate of literacy as we've known it up to now. It's the concept of graceful degradation.

Graceful degradation is an important property of large networks:

> One of the original motivations for the development of the Internet by the Advanced Research Projects Agency (ARPA) of the U.S. government was the desire for a large-scale communications network that could resist massive physical as well as electronic attacks including global nuclear war. In graceful degradation, a network or system continues working to some extent even when a large portion of it has been destroyed or rendered inoperative.

> (Source: http://searchnetworking.techtarget.com/sDefinition/0,290660, sid7_gci1238360,00.html)

"Fault-tolerance or graceful degradation is the property of a system that continues operating properly in the event of failure of some of its parts," sums up Wikipedia. We prefer viewing the steady proliferation of applications and platforms with optimism rather than alarm. What's so bad about having a host of alternative failsafes for disseminating information? It's not as if we can control the definition of literacy, any more than we can control the outlets from which people take the words and images and sounds they've decided are worth their time and attention.

We probably aren't rearing a generation of scholars addicted to online sources only, and the thundering migration to myriad versions of online content by no means makes all printed content obsolete or even inferior. We're becoming a culture with many different sources of information; we have to become smart about the publishing tools and distribution channels available and use the best ones for the job. We have to broaden our definition of audience and of literacy—pluralizing both.

THE AGE OF INFORMATION: RICH BUT SCATTERED

One of the most intelligent analyses we've found is an article by Jonathan Follett, "Envisioning the Whole Digital Person" (Feb. 2007). Follett speaks of a rich but "scattered information environment" in which the search for valuable content is an important aspect of literacy—and information retrieval and storage are discretionary acts by individuals:

Our lives are becoming increasingly digitized—from the ways we communicate, to our entertainment media, to our e-commerce transactions, to our online research. As storage becomes cheaper and data pipes become faster, we are doing more and more online—and in the process, saving a record of our digital lives, whether we like it or not.

As a human society, we're quite possibly looking at the largest surge of recorded information that has ever taken place, and at this point, we have only the most rudimentary tools for managing all this information—in part because we cannot predict what standards will be in place in 10, 50, or 100 years.

Our evolving digital existence has made it difficult to keep track of and control all of our information. People are executing more and more transactions online, but entities other than users govern the terms of many of these transactions. Within the digital world, there are items we might choose to share—like our videos, blogs, and playlists—and other items we would prefer to keep private—like our medical records, our financial transactions, and our personal communications. Our personal knowledge assets are scattered, haphazardly organized, and growing rapidly. As a result, we are struggling to access our data, organize it in a meaningful way, and interact with it....

Today, we can purchase storage media for one dollar a gigabyte or less. However, while we have the capability and capacity to save our data, that doesn't mean we do so with any set purpose in mind. The full impact of our having unlimited digital storage has not yet become apparent, because its existence as a commodity has so far been relatively short. But there is no doubt that a massive amount of personal information is accumulating on people's hard disks everywhere. The greatest piece of unmapped territory for the search industry to index may not be the dark data that resides on corporate servers, but rather people's rapidly growing personal archives.

Follett advises, "We should take a holistic view of the digital person." In short, we have our work cut out for us: "As designers of user experiences for digital products and services, we can make people's digital lives more meaningful and less confusing. It is our responsibility to envision not only techniques for sorting, ordering, and navigating these digital information spaces, but also to devise methods of helping people feel comfortable with such interactions. To better understand and ultimately solve this information management problem, we should take a holistic view of the digital person. While our data might be scattered, people need to feel whole."

Connectivity, community, collaboration: All give us more sources of information than we know what to do with. It can be difficult to decide what or whom to pay attention to—so much so that some people admit they're reading less than ever, in any medium. Which is why the fate of reading in

general and print media in particular—especially books—is considered ques-
tionable. We beg to disagree. Yes, the fate of content not worth its salt is
sealed, and we should thank the impatience of the Internet culture for that.
Print isn't a magic medium—there's lots of swill on paper. Valuable content in
any medium will find its audience.

No, that's not quite right. Audiences will find valuable content, as defined
by themselves for themselves. Our job is to get out of their way.

3

Connecting with Tomorrow's Readers, Customers, and Colleagues

Who are "today's readers"? Well, in a sense, they're tomorrow's readers. If you're reading this book, chances are you're aware of the growing Internet influence on our world. Boomers, their kids, and many of their parents have adapted pretty well to it. But the generation now entering college and the workforce is the first to grow up with the Internet as a fact of life—a medium to be taken for granted the way the morning newspaper once was.

Whether you are working with them; selling to them; trying to inspire, educate, or entertain them; or just need their cooperation—no matter what field you're in, you will need to interact and communicate with these so-called *millennials*. They are the new audience.

The first thing to understand about them is this: They are not heir to the indifference and cynicism of Generation X-ers—so don't call them Generation Y, if you want to be thought au courant.

To help writers, editors, and publishers create content that will appeal to the millennials, particularly those born between 1980 and 2002, we begin with the basics: a psychographic profile of this age group, tips for interacting with them, and pointers to generational trends that will affect every industry.

WHO ARE THE MILLENNIALS?

The problem of information overload has become a cliché to this new generation of speedy and willing multitaskers. Parents are astonished to find their children sitting on the couch watching television, texting e-mail to friends, surfing the Web, and glancing at a textbook. All at the same time, with no signs of feeling stressed.

Far from being disorganized, millennials are accomplished at focusing selectively and making rapid decisions. They have adapted to a culture that is so fast-paced it requires them to pull the most important information out of a given medium and move on. And keep moving.

Millennials can't remember a time when their home did not have one computer or several. They use the Internet as an extension of themselves—and not just for e-mail. In fact, there's evidence that e-mail isn't immediate enough for this generation. They like to send and get information via text messaging, RSS feeds, wikis, and blogs. To meet their expectations, we have to become familiar with the vocabulary that reflects the new-media landscape.

As reported in a *Chronicle of Higher Education* article (January 5, 2007) about a technology forum the newspaper sponsored, millennials "have grown up with more choices and more selectivity in the products and services they use, which is why they do not have, for example, a generational music." Imagine—an entire generation not defined by music!

With the advent of Web sites like Pandora.com, millennials are exposed to a much wider range of styles and artists than the music played on the weekly Top 40. And that's not limited to *new* music. Elvis Presley Enterprises reports that more than a third of visitors to Graceland are under the age of 35. The advent of satellite radio allows this generation to pick and choose what music they want to listen to.

WHAT DO MILLENNIALS VALUE?

Until 9/11, the millennial generation experienced the most economic prosperity of any generation. Generally speaking, they're still used to a relatively fabulous lifestyle. Most millennials have never had to share a car, let alone a bedroom. They have cell phones, iPods, extensive travel experience, and extravagant birthday parties. They are privileged, although they don't see themselves that way at all.

They love money. They love earning it, saving it, and spending it. Millennials save over a quarter of what they earn. The oldest members of this generation are only in their mid-20s, but 16 percent of them own stocks and bonds, and 7 percent own mutual funds. Millennials are spenders, too, but they know they need to save now so they can spend later. They expect to be paid well for their efforts in business—and they'll save hard and play hard with that money.

The *Chronicle* article summed up personal characteristics that accompany those values: "They rarely read newspapers—or, for that matter, books. They are impatient and goal-oriented. They hate busywork, learn by doing, and are used to instant feedback. They want it *now.* They think it's cool to be smart. They have friends from different ethnic backgrounds. They want flexibility—in the classroom and in their lives."

Well. So much for the patient, passive, polite Dear Readers of yesteryear! See the chart on page 21 for a cross-generational comparison.

COMPARATIVE MINDSETS OF LIVING GENERATIONS
Veterans & the "Silent Generation": 1901–1942
Baby Boomers: 1943–1960
Generation X: 1961–1980
Millennials: 1981–2002

	Veterans	Baby Boomers	Generation X	Millennials
Values	Loyalty Duty Patriotism	Individualistic Entrepreneurial Status-conscious	Education	Loyalty Honor Family
Characteristics	Fearless Risk-averse Idealistic Moral Trust in authority	Liberal Less religious Cynical Experimental Social climbers	Alienated Tech-savvy Insecure Challenge authority	Confident Social Appreciate diversity Goal-oriented Multitaskers
Sign of independence	No generational sign	Extension of house phone in own bedroom	Home computer	Cell phone with Internet access and texting capabilities
Communicating	Write me a letter	Write me a memo	E-mail me	Well, you can Facebook me, but it's probably faster to text
Fiscal philosophy	Don't spend what you don't have	Charge it!	Save it for a rainy day	Money is made to be spent
Leadership in business	Command and control	Climb the corporate ladder	Challenge others and authority	Collaborate
Mantra	Slow and steady wins the race	Keeping up with the Joneses	I can do it myself	Two heads are better than one

Millennials are special. They know this because their parents, teachers, tutors, guidance counselors, private soccer coaches, therapists, nutritionists, and nannies have told them so their entire lives.

They are confident; they expect good news and believe in themselves. In an age of highly publicized child kidnappings and other risks to young people, millennials have been kept from harm's way and lead highly structured (or, as some child psychologists have suggested, overscheduled) lives.

Millennials have attended schools where collaboration is the norm and competition is toned down. The *Chronicle* technology forum moderator, Richard T. Sweeney, noted that "to get this generation involved, you have to figure out a way to engage them and make their learning faster at the end of the day." A student participant explained, "When a teacher is lecturing to you in the front of the room, it's really boring. You don't get involved, and you tend to kind of zone out the whole time. I need more bells and whistles to keep my attention."

Universities are recognizing this trend more quickly than corporations. When most universities were still mainly lecturing to students, Furman University in Greenville, SC, was exploring "engaged learning" as a way to not only teach millennials but also "develop their self-confidence and sharpen their leadership skills." In addition to collaborative student-teacher research projects, the school "emphasizes education outside the traditional classroom," aiming "to give students greater responsibility" for their learning experiences and encourage leadership. A significant number of Furman students participate in internships. Others serve as teaching apprentices on campus or in elementary and secondary schools. Almost a quarter enroll in study abroad programs sponsored by the university, and a majority work as volunteers for social service agencies or other helping programs in the Greenville community. For many Furman students, these out-of-class opportunities are life-changing experiences.

IMPORTANT INFLUENCES: TECHNOLOGY AND PARENTS

In a 2005 CNET article, "The Millennials Usher in a New Era," Stefanie Olsen wrote that millennials "are simply using today's technologies to express a sense of belonging that young people have always desired":

> By only their seventh birthday, most children in the United States will have talked on a cell phone, played a computer game and mastered a TV-on-demand device like TiVo, much to the amazement of technically challenged parents. By 13, researchers say, the same children will have gone through several software editions of instant messaging, frequented online chat rooms and downloaded their first illegal song from BitTorrent. College-age millennials will likely own a laptop and take for granted ubiquitous broadband

Internet access. They may also be intimately familiar with the feeling of "highway hypnosis"—the ability to drive or multitask with little memory of the process of getting there.

Millennials are also experts at online social networking. Reflecting their acceptance of diversity, they use the new online communities to get out of their environment and into another city, country, or culture with the click of a mouse. The exponential growth of online social networking tools such as Facebook, MySpace, YouTube, Flickr, and others has transformed the way college students and young adults meet new people and keep in touch with each other. (For more about the phenomenon of social networking, see chapters 4 and 5.)

Because such sites have become gathering places for young people, they draw traffic from those who want to communicate with them:

- Penn State's online news site, The Digital Collegian, reported that a professor is leading the trend in putting course information on Facebook. He believes that he'll reach more students by taking the course to their turf.
- The University of Kansas has used YouTube to post promotional videos, also believing that it's smart to go where the kids already are.
- Some politicians are purchasing advertising space and creating their own profiles on social networking sites, reaching hundreds of thousands of 18- to 24-year-olds, a group whose voting turnout has always been low.

Many students feel a false sense of security with social networking, which carries some real risks. Student profiles are searchable only by people within the same school and peers who have been "accepted" as friends, so millennials feel they "know" the people with whom they are networking—though academia is not a crime-free zone.

But technology also allows them to stay in touch with parents more easily than ever before. It's not uncommon for millennials to talk to each parent daily, sometimes multiple times. Have you heard the term *helicopter parents*? They're hovering protectively and they're here to stay. Parents of millennials tend to have planned for a smaller family and to base their sense of self-worth on the success of their children. Older and highly educated, they are often thrilled to see their little millennials move back home after college.

This is a true story: Two girls were asleep one night in their sorority house when they woke to the sound of glass breaking. Terrified, they listened at the door and became convinced that an intruder had broken in downstairs. One of the girls grabbed her cell phone and called...her mother, 500 miles away. The mother called the police on another line while staying on the cell phone with her daughter.

Universities are creating "parent relations departments." Professors still get pleas to raise a student's grades after they're issued, but now it's often the parents doing the pleading—or demanding. Extreme examples of helicopter parents are those who attend job interviews with or for their children and conduct salary negotiations.

But there's a positive side to the helicopter parent phenomenon. Remember the healthy millennial ego and sense of optimism? Fewer millennials are from broken homes—divorce rates are down for their parents—and drug and alcohol abuse, unplanned pregnancies, and abortion rates are declining among them. In fact, they frown on promiscuity and swearing, even as these are encountered to extremes in pop culture. (Didn't see that coming, did you?)

INTERACTING WITH MILLENNIALS

Just as technology and the information it conveys change daily, so do the rules for working and communicating with other people. This is especially true with millennials. Above all, remember that they are highly educated and motivated, and they pressure themselves to succeed. They expect the very best from colleagues, commercial transactions, and the causes they champion in their free time.

When You're Working with Them...

Claire Raines, in her book *Beyond Generation X: A Practical Guide for Managers*, published a list of the ways managers drive their millennial employees crazy. Ignoring input and feedback from employees, giving virtually meaningless raises, and failing to give regular performance reviews ranked high. To build relationships with millennials, she offers the following advice:

- **Give feedback, both instant and regular.** Millennials have spent years getting immediate attention from parents and immediate responses from the Internet. They want to know how they are doing, where the benchmark is, and how they can improve.
- **Give them only what they need to know.** As high-tech as this generation is, millennials don't respond very well to online learning. While Gen X-ers communicated through very pragmatic data, easily relayed online, millennials are more likely to respond to information that is presented in other ways than charts and graphs, such as real-life stories, collaborative projects, and the Socratic method. Better to hold a meeting than send an e-mail with many attachments.
- **Forget about expecting them to "pay their dues."** This is a generation that did not have to start at the bottom. They're special, remember? They

won't understand why you expect an entry-level associate to get the coffee, and they certainly won't like it. Changing jobs doesn't have the same stigma it used to. Millennials will just find another job where they can contribute more than an afternoon latte run.

- **Allow them to collaborate.** Millennials grew up in a learning culture of working together on group projects and other assignments. Figure out a way to fit working groups into your corporate culture. Create "pods" of people who work creatively together.

- **Do not give them busywork.** You'll get more out of your millennials by sending them home an hour early than by keeping them busy till 5 p.m. collating and stapling. Busywork builds resentment in this generation, for whom a major motivation is making a true contribution.

- **Pay them well.** Millennials see their paycheck as a benchmark of their success. If you don't pay them well, expect high turnover. These highly motivated and overachieving young adults will leave your company faster than you can imagine. As Claire Raines noted, puny raises do nothing but annoy millennials.

- **Show that they are making a contribution.** Give your millennials tangible ways to make a difference at your company. They value loyalty and service. Teach them that they can be heroes at your organization, and they will work very hard for you.

- **Understand that they will most likely leave**—and after a relatively short time. Millennials are pursued as employees, and they are always looking for the next best thing. They aren't used to paying their dues, so the baby boomer style of climbing the ladder is foreign to them. While they're with you they're loyal, but don't take it personally when they move on to more responsibility, a bigger paycheck, or simply a different experience at another company. If you want to keep them, promote them before someone else can.

When You're Selling to Them...

Millennials have highly sensitive bull-detection radar. They're suspicious of marketing, and with reason. Advertisements and marketing campaigns have always come at them from every direction. So how do you market to a generation that's oversaturated with marketing?

- **Accept it: They're not like you.** Tips for communicating with millennials published by MindPowerInc.com included this one: "They're more technologically advanced, so your message might be squarely on target, but if it's in the wrong media, the millennials will never hear it. They want a choice of all types of communication." That means Web sites, instant messaging (IM), gaming, iPods, and, yes, traditional print materials.

- **Integrate your advertising.** You won't reach the millennials through TV alone. Think Facebook, podcasts, and on-campus word-of-mouth when you're crafting a communications strategy.
- **Don't patronize them.** Millennials know how to see through the fluff and pick out what's real and relevant. Slick printed brochures with no substance won't get a second look from them.
- **But they *can* be marketed to.** Reaching them will mean thinking outside the boxes—as in televisions and radios. Members of this generation will skip any ad they can, and their TiVo and iPods eliminate the commercials. But they do research—usually online—before buying a product, so pay attention to how your product is being talked about online.
- **Don't underestimate the power of friendship.** Millennials think of friends as family. They listen to their peers regarding, well, pretty much everything. As a marketer, your goal should be to make your product the one everyone is talking about. Whether that means creating a Facebook group, recruiting campus representatives, or using viral marketing, make sure that friends are telling friends about your product.

When You Need Their Voluntary Support...

Perhaps you work for a political campaign and need to get out the vote. Or maybe you want to mobilize young adults for a service project. Possibly you're starting a company and can only afford to hire entry-level millennials for the job.

- **Use their talents.** These tech-savvy young adults have energy and knowledge that older people may not possess. Don't just give them busywork like sealing envelopes; let them use their skills to help you. Most likely you'll get a great return on your investment.
- **Tell them how they can add to their resume.** Millennials want to know where they are going and how to get there. Entice them by showing how they could highlight their experience on a resume.
- **Allow them to work in teams.** Never forget the culture of collaboration. Place them in a group together, and you may be thrilled to find them finishing projects early and asking for new ones.
- **Listen to them.** Those helicopter parents have been listening to millennials' opinions and preferences about absolutely everything, so this generation expects to be taken seriously. While they may have a lot to learn, you might also get some good ideas from them.
- **Provide a fun environment.** Millennials are social. They like meeting new people and are confident in new surroundings. Make sure they have some fun time. They also mesh well with older generations, so give them a chance to get to know everyone in your organization.

Psychographics is not an exact science, and no generational profile can pin-point the traits of every person. But by paying attention to generational shifts, we can align our message strategies for the people we most need to reach in publishing today: tomorrow's content creators, readers, and thought leaders. The millennials feel quite at home in our diverse, global, interactive, wired (or, more accurately for some, wireless) culture. Want to encourage millennials to listen to and engage with you? Return the favor.

4

Understanding What Web 2.0 Means for Editors and Writers

As you read this, another in the series of digital tsunamis will have passed over, receding to expose corroded printing presses and people scrubbing ink out of their sleeves. The water is still icy, particularly in a place like Stockholm on the Baltic, where, on January 1, 2007, the world's oldest continuously published newspaper, *Post Och Inrikes Tidningar*, departed print forever to go online. The paper, whose name translates as *Mail and Domestic Tidings*, was first published in 1645 by Queen Kristina to keep her subjects informed of affairs of state.

The pundits advised not to read too much into this: *POIT* is the official Swedish publication for bankruptcies and corporate and government announcements. Still...362 years. What is relevant for this discussion is how the news of the repositioning was reported. The Poynter Institute for Media Studies quoted a spokesperson from *POIT* who described the transition as "a natural step." In the UK's *Guardian*, however, a different spokesperson lamented the change as "a cultural disaster." Time will tell whether circulation will be greater for the online version, which is the goal of its publishers.

The leaders of far younger, more comprehensive publications have also been taking the plunge, carrying their editors and writers with them. Nowhere is this truer than along the Hudson River, where *New York Times* publisher Arthur Sulzberger Jr. is carrying not only a newsroom of recalcitrant editors and other word people with him but also the future of a great news organization and probably of other newsrooms as well, to say nothing of the communities they have long served.

Asked by a reporter at the 2007 World Economic Summit in Davos, Switzerland, if the *Times* would still be printed on paper in five years, Sulzberger responded, "I really don't know whether we'll be printing the *Times* in five years, and you know what? I don't care, either." It takes only a few minutes of Web browsing to find sentiments similar to these from the leaders of media companies that have had newspapers, books, or magazines at the center of their work.

Colin Crawford, president and CEO of International Data Group's *PCWorld* and *Macworld*, wrote in his blog in early 2007: "Going forward, IDG Communications will define itself as a Web-centric information company.... In the past, media organizations controlled content and pushed it out to subscribers; today's media has to deal with a world of social connections, networking, and collective actions enabled by the Internet."

Crawford predicted, "The more enlightened in our media world will figure how to allow their audiences freedom to create and share their knowledge and content and to mash it up in a way that engages users. We have to become facilitators as much as content creators. Our brands are trusted—they have quality content and loyal audiences—these are our competitive advantages, but we'll only hold onto those assets if we truly listen to our communities and provide appropriate environments for user-initiated conversations and user-created content."

Other publishers entering the freezing tide surely noted Crawford's comment that, for the first time, online revenues for the multifaceted IDG passed its print revenues.

WHAT WEB 2.0 WILL LOOK LIKE

The shorthand term for the next-Internet-age phenomenon envisioned is "Web 2.0." Crawford says it will be characterized by "social connections, networking, and collective actions." It will allow audiences "freedom to create and share...and to mash it up." It will be fueled by "user-initiated conversations and user-created content."

Crawford speaks as a part of a well-entrenched content enterprise whose professionals and processes are going through transitions that other professionals are also experiencing, to varying degrees, across the entire publishing spectrum. *POIT*, the *New York Times*, and IDG were not the only publishing enterprises in transformation in 2006. Consider how far the tsunamis have rolled inland:

- Knight-Ridder sold its newspapers and disappeared from the business.
- Gannett morphed its newsrooms into "information centers."
- The *Washington Post* took down the wall between print and online newsrooms.
- Seven newspaper groups brought Yahoo into the fold, with much trepidation.
- About.com, the collection of very specialized Web sites acquired by the *New York Times*, was the company's best revenue producer.

- Blogs continued their explosive growth, and many gained journalistic credibility.
- The term *crowdsourcing* actually came to mean something.

In 2006, the American Press Institute undertook the NewspaperNEXT project, a yearlong effort to test business models that will, the Institute said, help the entire industry confront "the disruptive changes that threaten (newspapers') current way of doing business with no clear future path."

The phrase "no clear future path" is a disturbing statement from an industry that has been adjusting to digital alternatives since well before the Web became universal and that has, in effect, led the information industry as a whole.

But, as the examples above illustrate, news organizations now have to contend with millions of people, many of whom are former loyal readers, moving across the landscape with cell phones, laptops, digital cameras, iPods, and BlackBerrys in hand, inventing *citizen journalism* and tossing out *user-generated content* like kudzu.

Did the news industry miss something in those years of trial and error? It's not so much what the traditional media leaders missed as what they could not—or would not—believe. And that is (unbelievably) that *the medium is the message.*

The medium for digital information is a collection of networked computers; more precisely, networked digital resources that include software programs and the information they manage. Most important are the numbers of people who are adept at making use of the information and the applications.

The computers at the heart of this medium are subject to Moore's Law, which means a steady procession of more power, more storage, and faster data transmission. In practice, this means a steady procession of capabilities, from text-based e-mail accessible by only a comparative few in the 1980s to a cell phone video of a tyrant's hanging accessible by millions in 2006. It's just computing power, after all.

The message inherent in this medium is contrary not only to the mentality of traditional print-based publishing but to the entire value proposition behind it. The "Information Age" has long been a misnomer; since the earliest days of 300 baud e-mail, we have been in an "Information-Sharing Age." And the essence of the medium is collaboration. As a *Business Week Online* commentator observed in mid-2005: "For the first time in human history, mass cooperation across time and space is suddenly economical."

It is this "mass cooperation" that brings us back to the rapidly expanding universe that is Web 2.0. MySpace, Facebook, YouTube, and Wikipedia are the great exemplars of mass cooperation in the market today. That cooperation exists in the constant refreshing of information coming into these sites from millions of users and the involvement of readers in rating, selecting, and forwarding their favorites and sharing them with their friends.

These sites—and eBay and Amazon—are designed for harnessing the collective intelligence of their users. This is a core principal of Web 2.0 applications development—functionality for users is built into the software design. It is incumbent on contemporary publishers to infuse their operations with such attributes.

In a 2005 paper, leading technology publisher Tim O'Reilly described the functional principles of Web 2.0 as primarily the qualities and attributes of the Web platform itself (rather than of Web users), so they're somewhat technical. But O'Reilly's description implies that editorial and creative thinkers can put the principles to use, so they're worth considering:

- **The long tail.** Small sites make up the bulk of the Internet's content; narrow niches make up the bulk of the possible applications. *Therefore*: Leverage customer self-service to reach out to the entire Web, to the edges and not just the center, to the long tail and not just the head.
- **Data are the next Intel Inside.** Applications are increasingly data-driven. *Therefore*: For competitive advantage, seek to own a unique, hard-to-recreate source of data.
- **Users add value.** The key to competitive advantage in Internet applications is the extent to which users add their own data to that which you provide. *Therefore*: Don't restrict your "architecture of participation" to software development. Involve your users both implicitly and explicitly in adding value to your application.
- **Network effects by default.** Only a small percentage of users will go to the trouble of adding value to your application. *Therefore*: Aggregate user data as a side-effect of their use of an application.
- **Some rights reserved.** Intellectual property protection limits re-use and prevents experimentation. *Therefore*: When benefits come from collective adoption, not private restriction, make sure that barriers to adoption are low. Follow existing standards, and use licenses with as few restrictions as possible. Design for "hackability" and "remixability."
- **The perpetual beta.** When devices and programs are connected to the Internet, applications are no longer software artifacts, they are ongoing services. *Therefore*: Add new features on a regular basis as part of the normal user experience. Engage your users as real-time testers, and measure how people use the new features.
- **Cooperate, don't control.** Web 2.0 applications are built on a network of cooperating data services. *Therefore*: Offer Web service interfaces and content syndication, and re-use the data services of others.

- **Software above the level of a single device.** The PC is no longer the only access device for Internet applications, and applications that are limited to a single device are less valuable than those that are connected. *Therefore*: Design your application to integrate services across handheld devices, PCs, and Internet servers.

The point of this somewhat extensive list is to illustrate the atmosphere in which content and information will inevitably pass as they find places, and reincarnations, in the hands of end users. The separation between creation and distribution has narrowed so completely in digital space that it is often hard to detect at all.

EDITING USER-GENERATED CONTENT

Perhaps the primary irony arising from the dramatic expansion of user-generated content and sharing capabilities—even as the wonders of Web 2.0 are unfolding—is a new demand for more and better intercession or intermediation. What we might otherwise call...an editorial presence! Let's consider two current expressions of collaborative content creation with different editorial models.

- **Iraqslogger.com**, a commercial enterprise, stands out among the many sites and blogs covering or commenting on the Iraq war. It is run by a former head of CNN News, Jordan Eason, who explains: "Our network is a combination of personal relationships, reliable sources on the ground, experience in the region, insight into events, and discreet and well-placed sources inside government, industry and a wide spectrum of political groups. Information, news, analysis and safety alerts are generated 24/7 by our staff in the US, Europe and Iraq." This worldwide cadre of news sources gives the site wide and deep coverage of topics—such as Kirkuk Police Blotter, Iraq Black Market, Oil, and Contractors—that go uncovered by most media, new and old alike. Iraqslogger.com has harnessed the creative elements supported by the Web into an ordered, edited resource with high journalistic standards—but with a business model that is entirely dependent on collaboration. Soon clients will pay for variations of its byproducts.
- **Wikipedia** worries some content professionals because of the insane objective of its cofounder, Jimmy Wales: "Wiki is an effort to create and distribute a multilingual free encyclopedia of the highest possible quality to every single person on the planet in their own language." "Free" and "highest possible quality" don't fit comfortably into the same sentence, do they? Wikipedia entries are created by the whims, interests, and expertise of persons who are unknown to almost everyone. The topics, writing, and

editing depend on open collaboration, constrained only by a few rules of
engagement and the rare intervention of the owners if peer editing does
not correct known misinformation or hoaxes.

Like blogs or the content management systems involved in running a newspaper, a wiki is simply a platform for assembling information and an idea for
making it available. Wikipedia is just one expression of that idea, followed
now by other variations in various stages of readiness: Wiktionary,
Wikiquote, Wikibooks, Wikisource, Wikimedia Commons, Wikispecies,
Wikinews, and Wikiversity.

Iraqslogger.com and Wikipedia both illustrate an important point in the
evolution of content creation, editing, and reading. The first model supplies
editorial context and rigor to news and analysis provided by a diffuse network
of professionals, on whose collaboration the value of the site depends. The
second model allows a body of content to appear and be refined (written and
edited) over time by volunteers (readers), on whose collaboration the value of
the work depends.

Even though good old *Post Och Inrikes Tidningar* in Sweden will still serve
the bureaucrats and lawyers, as it has since 1645, it is in a better position as a
Web-only resource to engage its users, collaborate with them in the creation
of new and valuable content forms, and harness their collective wisdom. As
such capabilities are put in place, it is easy to see how important editorial
intermediation will remain, long after the last press has stopped rolling.

And writers and editors will be the recipients of scores of tools that mate-
rialize, like Orks, out of the mud of the Web 2.0 pool, rich with past conventions and future inspiration. Be not faint of heart.

5

Listening to People Talk:
How Conversational Media Works

Mere publishing is no longer good enough—not if you really want to succeed online and elsewhere. These days, people are doing far more than reading or otherwise passively absorbing content online.

Online forums have become a theater of engagement: How often and well you engage with others, and how open you are to what others have to say, largely determine how much you get noticed and gain influence. This is why, increasingly, it's useful to think of online media as *conversational media*.

WHAT "CONVERSATIONAL MEDIA" MEANS

The definition of *conversational media* is using the Internet (or any electronic medium) to publicly converse with other people. This generally happens through online tools such as blogs (Web logs), forums, e-mail discussion lists, chat rooms, wikis, podcasts, virtual meeting services, social media (such as Digg.com), photo- or video-sharing sites (such as YouTube.com), virtual environments (such as SecondLife.com), and whatever else the Internet will have dished up by the time you read this.

Conversational media don't necessarily live on the Internet, though they seem to work best there. Some offline examples of conversational media include phone seminars, talk radio, and letters sent to the editor of a print publication (a limited and primitive, yet occasionally still powerful, type of conversational media).

The Internet is a boon to conversational media because it provides the greatest potential reach for public conversations: across geography, communities, and time. It also allows more people than ever to join the public conversation with few or no restraints on how they participate—for better and for worse.

These are "public conversations" in that they're available to some sort of *community*, not just to the individuals who are actively conversing. A community can be totally open and public, like most blogs are. It also can be private or semiprivate talk on an intranet, a members-only e-mail discussion list, or a media-sharing site such as Flickr.com, which is good for family/friends-only content.

Conversational media overlap with other forms of communication—they're a moving target. Any conversational forum is defined partly by the people who voluntarily participate, the technology that supports them, and the community's sponsor or host. Or that's how Gahran thinks about conversational media.

"Other people often disagree with me vigorously," she admits on her blog on the subject, RightConversation.com. For instance, a fellow veteran journalist, on hearing how Gahran defines *conversational media*, protested, "E-mail lists are not media! They're just people talking!" Gahran says alternative views are fine with her: "One thing I deeply enjoy about conversational media is how fundamentally *human*—and therefore subjective—this kind of communication is."

"CONVERSATIONAL STYLE" TIPS

Conversational media allow an intimacy that makes them feel spontaneous and vital, but—as for any kind of publishing—certain conventions apply.

- **Keep the personal front and center.** Try as you may, you can't converse with "an audience" any more than you can wage war on "terror." There really are no collective identities, only people. *Audience* is an abstract concept of convenience, not a reality of communication. Therefore, when you use conversational media, embrace your personal identity. It's important to use your name—don't bury yourself behind a corporate or other amorphous identity. Presenting yourself as an authentic individual encourages engagement and builds credibility. You can't have a conversation without people in it, and you're one of those people. So speak in the first person, mention personal experiences as appropriate, and generally speak on a human scale.
- **Picture the people you're conversing with online.** Better yet, picture *just one* person. This can be a real person you know (or know of) or an imaginary individual who personifies the community you're trying to connect with. In your mind, give this person a face, a name, a voice, a personality, and at least some background or context. What mood is he or she in? What does this person already know, believe, or feel about you or what you wish to discuss? Envision this person standing next to you or sitting across from you. You're not on stage, and the other person is not part of an audience. You're both just hanging out, on an equal footing.
- **Use the second person freely.** As you get involved in an online conversation, say *you* more than you might when writing a typical business or pro-

fessional document. The second person is a neat little psychological trick: It implies that you're speaking directly to a person. People naturally find this more engaging than being treated like part of a faceless audience. That's just how our brains are wired. Like motion in your peripheral vision, hearing *you* is attention-grabbing. Don't believe me? The next time you post something online, try saying "Maybe you think" instead of using more remote language such as "Some might think" or "One might think." Give people a way to respond to your statement publicly (as a blog comment) or privately (via an e-mail link). More people than usual will respond.

DON'T START CONVERSATIONS FROM SCRATCH

Often, when people first learn about conversational media (especially blogging, which is currently very popular), their first thought is "Well, our organization needs a blog." So they add a blog to their site, because it's so easy to do. And they post to it. They watch their site statistics and are dismayed that the blog receives few visitors. Even more discouraging, no one leaves comments. Eventually, the postings get less frequent, and then the blog is abandoned. From then on, the organization is down on blogging. "We tried it, and it doesn't work."

What went wrong? They tried to start a new conversation from scratch, before building bridges with existing relevant communities. Let's dispel the most unfortunate and pervasive myth about conversational media: *If you build it, they will come.* That fallacy has caused many people to start backwards in conversational media, become discouraged, and miss opportunities.

In online media, especially conversational media, community is golden. A strong, vibrant, positive community is like a bank where people mutually store and increase their energy, knowledge, and abilities. The sum becomes much greater than the parts. Everything is easier when there's community support and enthusiasm. And conversation is the gateway to any community.

Think about it—it's just common sense: You always find it easier to join a conversation than to start one, don't you? Imagine that you've arrived at a party. Lots of people are there already, and many of them are gathered in groups having conversations. You want to engage these people, to build relationships with them and gain a reputation among them. Which is the smarter approach?

- Float around the edges of the groups and get a sense of the ongoing conversations. When you find one that's interesting to you, join in.
- Stand in the center of the room and announce, "Okay, I'm here. You can come talk to me now."

The easiest and best way to get started in conversational media is to find relevant communities and join their conversations *before* you put much effort into launching your own blog, forum, or other conversational media initiative. That way, when you're ready to move forward with your project, you'll have the energy, support, and momentum of those communities to propel you toward your goals. Also, you'll have a better idea of what kind of initiative is likely to succeed.

Here's how that works:

- **Clarify your goals.** Figure out which communities you wish to engage, and why.
- **Find where those people gather online.** Which blogs do they read and—especially—comment on? Which forums do they frequent? Usually communities solidify around a few influential persons or organizations. If you're not sure where these thought leaders are, ask some people who represent the communities you seek to engage. If you ask enough people, you'll get recommendations. Remember, you're looking to connect with communities, not just to find resources on topics. For instance, if you wish to engage with lawyers, look for a venue where lawyers comment rather than one that covers legal topics.
- **Voraciously observe for at least a few days.** Read *everything* published on that blog or forum for a little while before you speak up. How active is that venue? What topics come up? How quickly do topics change? Do the bloggers or forum leaders engage in direct discussions with community members via comments? What's the tone or culture of that community?
- **Start contributing.** After a few days of observing, watch for a thread that resonates with you. That's your chance to speak up. Offer a constructive, relevant response that shows that you've been listening. Ideally, your first few contributions should be brief and not directly self-promotional.
- **Be patient.** Expect that most or all of your initial contributions will generate little or no response. Generally, newcomers need to gain a bit of a track record before people will engage with them.

Once you've established connections with communities through a few key blogs or forums, it's time to start putting more effort into your own blog or other conversational venue.

STRATEGIC COMMENTING

When you start your own blog (or forum, podcast, or other venue), it's easier and more fun to do it in a way that *honors and complements* the established online communities you've already joined. Pick up on what they're discussing, and expand those discussions on your blog. Eventually, you'll foster a unique new community that will help you achieve your goals.

The best way to build your own community, I've found, is strategic commenting. Here's how you do it:

- **Keep following—and participating in—the communities you've joined.** Conversational media are never just about your site. From the start, always make time to stay involved with relevant communities.

- **Write a couple introductory posts** explaining who you are and what your goals are. Don't conceal anything major. For instance, if you're writing a blog on behalf of a company that makes and sells organic pasta, say so. If you're running for the state legislature, say so. If you're an MD, say so. Indicate which topics you hope to discuss, and who you hope to engage in conversation. Label these posts with a category called "About me" or "About this blog," so people can find them easily.

- **Post your take on a lively ongoing discussion** currently happening in one or more communities. Go into your unique perspective or contribution in some detail, for at least three paragraphs or so. Be compelling and constructive. Make sure you reference—and link to, if possible—the ongoing discussions. (As long as they're public, that is. Never violate the boundaries of a private community.) End your post by asking people what they think. Simply asking the question is a great nudge to action.

- **Go back to where the discussion started, and leave a comment.** Thank the people who started the original discussion for making you think and inspiring you to write—everyone likes to be appreciated. Then briefly summarize the main point of your own blog posting. In that comment, include a direct link to your posting, and invite people to read and comment. You might write something like this: "Thanks for mentioning that people should periodically check their spare tire, Jane. That can be a lifesaver if you get a flat in a remote location. I also write about auto maintenance and safety. After I read your post, I decided to post a short set of step-by-step instructions in my blog explaining how to check your spare tire. You can find my posting at http://autosafety.com. I'd love it if you'd look it over and see if you have anything to add."

When you comment strategically, here's what can happen:

- You'll probably attract some new readers each time you do this, even if they don't respond with comments. Watch your site statistics.
- You may get some valuable cross-blog conversation going with more established bloggers.

- You'll be creating inbound links to your blog content. Search engines will notice this, and it could improve your ranking.
- You'll build a reputation as a constructive, engaging, helpful participant in the public conversation—and possibly as an expert in your field.
- Community leaders may start reading your blog and linking to you.
- You'll have fun. That's allowed! It's always more fun to have a conversation than to simply publish. This can motivate you to post more, and to read and comment on other blogs more.

Granted, as with any strategy, strategic commenting won't work every time. Often you'll get no acknowledgment or response, and sometimes it may even backfire a bit. Just roll with it. If you keep it up, it *will* succeed, and it will definitely build your reputation—and important community relationships— over time.

CUTTING THROUGH THE CONVERSATIONAL CLUTTER

In most conversational media, the big trick is cutting through the clutter. There's a *lot* of conversation happening at any time on any topic. The best way to increase the chance that people will want to read what you have to say is to give your contributions strong, clear titles.

Here, *title* can mean the title of a blog post, but the same guidelines generally apply to subject lines for postings to e-mail lists or Web forums, titles for podcast episodes, wiki pages, shared videos or photos, and so on.

Your titles must speak for themselves, because one thing you can count on online is that your titles *will* be displayed out of context. For instance, your titles will appear in results from search engines (like Google), in blog aggregators (like Technorati), in RSS feed readers, and in links from e-mail lists or other sites.

Here are my recommendations for writing effective, conversation-inducing titles:

- **Keep it short:** No more than 60 characters max, including spaces; and 25–40 is better.
- **Start with a content-rich word.** Avoid starting with "the," "this," "it," or similar generic words. Pick a word or phrase that refers directly to the main topic or point of your post. For instance, "Peanut Butter Perfection in Chicago" is a stronger title than "The Best Peanut Butter in Chicago." This makes your title stand out from a list. It seems stronger because it requires less mental processing to interpret. Also, this technique can improve how search engines (whether for the Web, or for a particular site or venue) rank your post. It's okay to lead with a strong phrase, use a colon as a separator, and finish with your point.

- **Use strong verbs.** Verbs convey action, and a sense of action and energy encourages people to pay attention. Try to work an active verb into your title. Avoid passive verbs. Also, choose the most specific verb you can. English is a rich language—don't be afraid to use it! For instance, "Franco Launches School Board Campaign" is a more visceral—and thus engaging—title than "Franco's School Board Campaign."
- **Pose a question.** This is a peculiarly effective way to leverage human psychology to engage a community in conversation. When you pose a question, people immediately start thinking in terms of responses. A blog post titled "Why Are My Tomatoes Dying?" is more likely to attract comments than "My Tomatoes Are Dying."

ARE YOU LISTENING, TOO?

If you're having trouble building bridges with online communities, your listening skills might need some work. There's no shame in that—most of us don't listen nearly as well as we should, nor do we indicate adequately that we're listening. To learn how to listen well, I recommend reading *The Lost Art of Listening* by Michael Nichols. While that book focuses on interpersonal relationships, the communication techniques it discusses apply perfectly to conversational media.

In conversational media, the people to whom you're listening probably won't know you're listening unless you reflect back to them your interpretation of what they said. Therefore, when you're leaving a comment or making a post in response to something someone has said, quote relevant lines before responding. An effective comment might read like this:

> Jean, you made some good points. In particular, you wrote, "I don't see why our city's zoning code doesn't allow some appropriate small commercial mixed in with residential. Why can't we have a corner grocery or coffee shop in my suburban neighborhood?" Historically, part of the reason for such policies has been concern over parking, but I think that doesn't reflect today's realities. Here's why...

This indicates to Jean (and everyone else who's actively or passively engaged in that conversation) that you heard what she said. You've also indicated your approval of the contributions to the conversation so far (by saying Jean made "some good points"). This signals your goodwill toward the community, your engagement, and your desire to be constructive.

This may seem like a nicety, but in fact it's quite important for encouraging people to engage in conversation with you, especially since the vast majority of people neglect this technique. We all hate feeling as though our words are scattering unheard into the void. Hearing even a small echo is encouraging.

SEEDING HIGH-QUALITY CONVERSATIONS

When you're just beginning to coalesce a community around your own conversational venue, it helps to reach out behind the scenes to insightful, articulate, or influential people and ask them to contribute to conversations. Some of the most successful bloggers I know (like Dave Taylor of the Intuitive Life Business blog: www.intuitive.com/blog) do this periodically to foster high-quality conversation and a diversity of voices.

Here's how it works:

- **Write a posting** on a topic that matters to you.
- **E-mail a few people after you publish the post.** Ideally, these should be people you know or have corresponded with. Mention your posting and summarize your main point. Then say something like this: *"I thought this post might interest you because [insert brief reason]. I respect your views on this topic and would very much like to hear what you have to say. If you have a moment, please stop by this post [give post URL] and leave a comment. Thanks."* Be sure to customize each request. Resist the temptation to copy several people on the same generic message. You'll be more likely to get responses if people know you took the time to reach out to them individually.
- **Comment back.** When you do receive high-quality comments, whether from people you invited to comment or from others, make sure to leave comments in response. Thank them for their contribution and, if possible, expand on it somehow or ask a question.
- **E-mail back.** Not everyone who leaves a comment will check back to see whether you've continued the conversation. Therefore, after you comment in response, take a moment to e-mail your high-quality commenters. Thank them for their contribution, and tell them you've responded publicly. Provide a direct link back to the post—or directly to the comment, if possible. Where will you get the e-mail address? Many comment systems collect this information. If yours doesn't, it probably allows the commenter to provide a URL. Usually if you follow that URL, you'll find an e-mail address there.

This process takes time, so don't feel obligated to do it with every post. However, it can pay off in several ways. By seeding your venue with high-quality comments, you set the tone for the kind of conversation you want to foster there. Thoughtful community members notice that and are then more likely to visit your venue—and even subscribe to your feed or e-mail alerts. Your venue will appear increasingly "worth the effort" it takes to make contributions, and increased community activity enhances the real and perceived value of your content.

This strategy can also yield valuable inbound links to your site. For instance, it's common for new bloggers to ask established bloggers to "trade links." It's safe to say that most established bloggers loathe and delete such requests, because they have nothing to do with substance or relevance.

But if you first participate constructively in the community around an established blog and later e-mail an invitation to the blogger to comment on something you've posted, you may get more than a comment. You may end up inspiring a posting in response that links to yours. That kind of "cross-blog conversation" is not only especially engaging but also provides a lasting benefit to your search engine ranking.

DETERRING POOR-QUALITY COMMENTS

Often bloggers complain about "worthless" or "inane" comments left on their sites. These range from off-topic blatherings to irrelevant questions to nice but useless "me too" replies. They aren't really comment spam (which, by the way, can largely be prevented with simple software tools); they just don't add any value and may dissipate the energy in a conversation.

Of course, any blog or forum manager can opt to moderate incoming comments. If your comment volume is fairly low, this is feasible; however, if you're trying to build community, routinely disapproving less valuable comments might not be your best move. Instead, try one or both of these approaches:

- **Encourage the meek.** Realize that many people who are new to conversational media—or tend to lurk rather than participate—may be self-conscious about speaking up. Shyness often lies behind supportive but inconsequential "me too" contributions. Therefore, when you have time, try to comment back to someone's meek comment with something like "Thanks for reading, and nice to see you here. I'd like to know more about your perspective on this. Do you have anything to add?" Then follow up with a behind-the-scenes e-mail to let them know that you've posted a blog response to their comment. About half the time this leads to greater engagement by a new community member.
- **Publish your comment policy.** It's perfectly reasonable to state that you moderate comments or that you may decline to publish off-topic or uncivil comments. Try to keep this policy simple. It's possible to establish boundaries or expectations in a friendly but not forbidding way. It's also fine to state that you may not have time to respond to all comments or that you reserve the right to correct spelling and other errors. The best place to publish a comment policy is immediately above or below where people enter comments.

EXPECT OCCASIONAL PROBLEMS

Conflict often is rooted in passion, and passion is a good thing in conversational media. At least, it *can* be a good thing. Especially strenuous disagreement.

But conversational media sometimes bring out the worst in people, from outright trolling (attempts to provoke you or your community), to "flame wars" (heated personal bickering or insults), to strenuous disagreements, to hurt feelings, to blatant misunderstandings. When this happens, there is always a solution.

Many people (especially those new to conversational media) don't know how to respond constructively to criticism or disagreement. If you're trying to build your reputation with a community, it helps to recognize these uncomfortable exchanges as opportunities to learn and grow, and to demonstrate that you respect the individuals who make up your community.

Say you've just received this comment from someone who's occasionally commented on your blog before:

> How could you possibly think that a national healthcare system might improve public health? I thought you understood a lot about healthcare until I read that.

Ouch! Yes, barbs like that always sting, and for many of us the first inclination is to strike back with a putdown, defensively restate the original case in stronger terms, or even delete the comment in a huff. It's crucial to pause—for an hour or two or maybe a day or two—and resist those destructive response options.

Remind yourself that this is an opportunity to build community. Remember that you don't know everything, that you don't own your community, and that you can't dictate what members should think. Then respond in a way that honors the passion and the perspective expressed while ignoring the negative tone in which it was delivered. Show that you're listening and that you're open to considering other viewpoints. Amy Gahran recalls what she overheard in a tai chi class: "The best self-defense is to have no self to defend."

To the prickly "how could you?" poster, you might respond,

> Thanks for offering an alternative perspective. I realize this is a controversial issue, and I know many people disagree with me. Obviously, you care deeply about the healthcare system and public health. I'd like to hear why you think a private healthcare system is necessary to support public health. I think we have an opportunity for an interesting discussion, and I'm always open to learning more.

By offering a gracious, welcoming response to snarky criticism, you turn the tables on your critic. Now the critic is on the defensive and under social pressure to respond civilly, if at all. You've shown tolerance and respect for diversity—conditions that make it safer for people to speak up in a community. You've also demonstrated strength and flexibility through restraint. Regardless of how the conversation continues or whether you and your critic learn from each other, as long as you stay calm and respectful, that's what people will remember about you.

Hosting a high-quality conversation often means not being "the expert" but being willing to allow others to influence you—within reason—and sometimes letting others have the last word.

KEEP THE CONVERSATION GOING

It's easy enough to get started in conversational media, but it's crucial to continue the conversation. Amy Gahran has agreed to dedicate a special section of her blog, The Right Conversation, to continuing this discussion. Go to eeicom.com/press/istyle. There you'll find an ongoing series of postings by Gahran that build on the ideas she's crystallized for us in this section—and she encourages you to "let your voice be heard."

6

Shaping Information for Its Users:
The Pursuit of Usefulness

A basic structural design underlies every kind of writing...[and] in most cases planning must be a deliberate prelude to writing. The first principle of composition, therefore, is to foresee or determine the shape of what is to come and pursue that shape.

—WILLIAM STRUNK JR. AND E. B. WHITE,
THE ELEMENTS OF STYLE

As Strunk and White pointed out long before anyone ever heard of "information architecture," all the written content we create must have some sort of structure. Whether it's straightforward data like population or crop production statistics, or more semantically rich information such as a corporate handbook or a biography, selecting an appropriate framework increases the odds that people will find it useful—which, after all, is the point.

The structure selected for any given writing project should reflect the goals of the intended audience for using the information. But we can go beyond responding to immediate wants and help readers (called *users* in this context) gain insights they didn't know they wanted—giving them a favorable perception that content is *usable.*

It's not merely a matter of organizing information so people can efficiently do what *we* intend them to. What will *they* want to be able to do with it? When communicators honor the potential for adding value to the reading (information access) experience, users repay them with attention.

LATCHING ON TO TOOLS

Only five useful structures are available to organize the factual and statistics-based information we publish in print and online, according to Richard Saul

Wurman, who lists them in his book *Information Anxiety 2* (Pearson Education, 2000) using the mnemonic LATCH: **L**ocation, **A**lphabet, **T**ime, **C**ategory, **H**ierarchy.

- **Location** can refer to geographic placement, such as you might find in a tourism guide or geography text. But it's also a structure used to explain such things as the layers of the atmosphere, the spatial characteristics of a building, and the layout of a Web page.
- **Alphabet** structure is most familiarly seen in the conventional way dictionaries, encyclopedias, and indexes are organized.
- **Time** is a natural organizational choice for narrating or listing a chronological sequence of events. It is seen in biographies and histories, programs of event activities, and descriptions of biological or administrative processes.
- **Categories** are a very versatile structure because they allow us to sort and group items or ideas by the characteristics we choose to highlight. For example, information about automobiles can be categorized by manufacturer, weight class, number of passengers, price range, and so forth. Categories can be nested as well, with subcategories within larger categories. The taxonomy used to classify living things—kingdom, phylum, class, order, family, genus, species—is a well-known example of a nested structure.
- **Hierarchy** is the structure most useful for rank-ordering or comparing items according to set criteria or on a scale. Cars can be ranked or compared according to their mileage, horsepower, or crash-test ratings. This is similar to the category structure, but the information is given a rank or weight on some sort of scale—biggest to smallest, richest to poorest, fastest to slowest.

MULTILATCHED CONTENT

Each of the basic LATCH structures can be used alone as an organizing aid, and certain structures seem to be naturally suited to certain types of content. But overreliance on deceptively simple defaults can ultimately be counterproductive, because users have different needs and preferences. For more user flexibility and better accessibility of multivariate content, we can use LATCH structures in combination.

For example, a state's tourism guide can be broken into regions, with information for the communities in each region alphabetized. An economic report can be organized by year, then by industry, or vice versa. The telephone directory once seemed permanently destined for an alphabetic structure; however, online, looking for a phone number and a name by entering an address (and vice versa) has broken that mold. Reverse dictionaries and thesauruses are not exclusively or strictly alphabetical; entries are categorically arranged.

A comparative review of baseball teams seems to naturally fit into a hierarchical structure, with teams and players ranked by their statistics—but reviewing the performance of one team's players might be best aided by an alphabetical list, so people can spot their favorites quickly. Biographies and histories fit into a time-based chronological structure—or do they? Award-winning biographers, historians, and creative-nonfiction authors have used fiction-writing techniques such as vignette and flashback to enrich their factual narratives.

Why mix techniques? Not only so content can be quickly searched but also to signal readers that it has been designed with their satisfaction in mind. In the age of information anxiety, reassuring readers that they're not wasting their time on irrelevant data or with an awkward design is just as important as the quality of the research and reporting.

VARY STRUCTURES FOR MULTIPLE VIEWPOINTS

So the basic organizational structures may fit certain situations well alone and others better in tandem. But each structure, by definition, imposes limits on how information can be used, and the perception of "easy access" is relative. Different users will have different viewpoints.

To take a familiar example, teachers frequently tell students who ask how a word is spelled to "look it up in the dictionary." This is good advice much of the time, but what if the student doesn't know how to even begin to spell the word? What about a word that is pronounced "kyoo?" Will that be found in with the Cs or Ks, or would the student know enough to look in the Qs? And what letter comes next? Assuming that some guesswork paid off, the student might find any one or all these different spellings—*cue*, *Kew*, and *queue*. The user has found information but hasn't found an answer.

Publishers have long recognized the information access problems inherent in default information structures and have tried to come up with different user-access schemes—primarily indexes and concordances. As they attempt to graft an alphabetic structure onto the existing structure, they can be helpful, but they aren't a cure-all for information usability and accessibility ills.

In addition to limiting how users *find* information, each structure constrains them to a certain *view* of the information. The very familiarity of default structures for different information types means that content organized using them can seem tiresome, which is perhaps why so many people avoid "looking it up" when it comes to spelling, assembly instructions, and so on.

As Wurman points out, when people look at information structured in an unexpected way, they can gain new insights: "Each vantage point, each mode of organization will create a new structure. And each new structure will enable you to see a different meaning, acting as a new method of classification from which the whole can be grasped and understood."

Marketers and population researchers have long known that much of the value in directory information is gained by looking at it in different structures. They put the raw information into databases and slice and dice it according to any number of logical organizing principles, such as by postal code (location) or by age, income, and other demographic divisions (categories and hierarchies). Each different way of looking at the data allows for different insights and types of knowledge that would otherwise be unavailable or very hard to ferret out.

That concept can be applied in many different ways. For example, my wife owns a set of gardening books divided into volumes according to the major categories of plants, such as annuals, perennials, trees and shrubs, bulbs, herbs and spices, vegetables, and so on. But the information in these volumes encompasses all the climate zones in North America, which sometimes makes finding advice specifically relevant to her garden a slow job of research.

We occasionally find ourselves having to discard some information that we've just taken time to read when we belatedly discover that it doesn't apply to our zone of need. The information in the gardening library might have been more usefully organized by climates, with focused information in each book for the gardeners in each zone.

This thought has evidently occurred to some authors and publishers; gardening books written for different climate zones, as well as for wet or dry conditions, gardening in cities or in the country, and so on, are available from publishers such as Rodale Press, Sunset Books, and Oxmoor House, as well as regional publishers and university presses.

Print publishers from other specialties have successfully taken on the challenge of using different structures for the same old information to provide different ways of looking at it and improving its usability. For example, O'Reilly Media, a publisher of technology books such as programming language reference guides, smashed the conventions of those books with its *Head First* series.

Among other innovations, these books use storytelling (a time-based structure) to explain different aspects of topics such as object-oriented design and the Java programming language. One wouldn't expect to read "Once upon a time..." in a programming book, but O'Reilly Media has won awards and, more important, praise from its audience for publishing books that work so effectively.

Publishers have also created visual dictionaries, designed to help people who know what a thing looks like but not what it's called. These dictionaries frequently use a category structure rather than an alphabetic one (and many are restricted to a particular field), so if we want to find out the name of the double-reed instrument that's bigger than an oboe, we'd begin by looking in the music category.

In addition, these innovative dictionaries help put otherwise isolated terms into context. Thus, we learn not only that the large double-reed is called a *bassoon* but also what the relative numbers of each type of instrument in a symphony orchestra are, as well as how they are arranged around the thing the conductor stands on (if we didn't already know, we'd learn that it's called a *podium*).

Such efforts are aimed not only at addressing the usability issues of the default LATCH structures but at giving users different insights into the subjects. Alternative structures might not be the most efficient in terms of getting the reader straight to the answer sought, but they lend themselves to the process of discovery. These alternative structures can help readers find out the thing they didn't know as well as guide them to things they didn't know that they didn't know. Some users welcome that sort of educational serendipity.

ONE DOCUMENT, MULTIPLE STRUCTURES

Online publishing opens up dramatic new ways to provide multiple structures for the same content, helping different users. Consider the collaborative online encyclopedia Wikipedia. We can begin by searching for a keyword or phrase, or by browsing one of the many subject area *portals* (a type of category structure). Because the reference is a hypertext, we can click a hyperlink to read related information, which can lead down a trail of related topics. For someone reading an article that includes a historical reference, a list of events that occurred on the same date or during the same year is a mouse click away, making it easy to see the historical context (a time structure).

The Internet Movie Database (imdb.com) is another good example of giving a wide variety of users multiple avenues for sorting through information. Looking for detailed information about a single movie or a comprehensive list of the movies an actor has performed in? A particular quote, or information about a movie production company? Users don't have to try to sift information from a structure designed as a static repository.

Designing a document or a collection of documents that allows users to approach from different directions, with different strategies, requires handling that information in different ways. And we can go beyond the basic concepts of hypertext, of linking one document to another. We can borrow some approaches and technologies from the realm of technical documentation to give our documents flexibility they haven't had before.

The constraints that technical writers work under have spurred the development of tools and systems that allow them to create multipurpose documentation; documentation that suits the needs of multiple audiences and that gives users several different ways of using it.

For example, although help systems comprise a set of discrete topics, each intended to stand as a separate chunk that provides self-contained information, they also often include the concept of a "browse sequence"; that is, a series of topics meant to be read in a certain order. Each topic in the browse sequence builds on the previous one and leads to the next topic. Many help authoring tools allow writers to define not just one but several browse sequences, to provide users with several possible paths through a text.

Many writing tools also have *conditional text* features that allow writers to selectively show or hide words, sentences, or paragraphs. A single set of source files can be a repository for a body of information from which you can build subsets of printed or online documents targeted at specific audiences.

For example, you could create a library of business law information, with some information flagged as applying to consumers, some to business owners, and some to both. From this library, you could use automated processes to create documents designed to answer a business owner's questions and a Web site with consumer information.

These tools also allow you to construct documents by picking from the various chunks of information. You can outline a table of contents and then— when you're ready to publish—the system builds the documents, including indexes, lists of tables, and other supporting information. Again, these can be documents destined for print or for publishing on the Web.

BUILDING BLOCKS AND FRAMEWORKS

The key to using any of these systems effectively comes back to how the information is structured: What will the building blocks, the chunks of information, be? What framework or frameworks can you put them together in?

In the arena of software documentation, the building blocks are usually descriptions of user interface elements, procedures, and underlying concepts. The frameworks usually include the various application modules and user roles (both of which are categories), and where a procedure fits in the workflow (location).

Other subject areas will have different building blocks and frameworks. We must ask ourselves whether these are the only building blocks, the only frameworks we can use. We also need to remember not just our goals for a document but our users' goals, as well.

In many cases, our goals and the users' overt goals will overlap; for example, their overt goal may be "Find out about X," while ours is "Inform people about X." However, users' goals aren't usually (if ever) limited to "Find out about X." In *About Face: The Essentials of User Interface Design* (IDG Books, 1995), Alan Cooper says that users' real goals often include things like not looking stupid, not making any big mistakes, getting work done, and having a bit of fun, "or at least not being too bored." Ideally, our designs should support these additional goals and not just the primary, overt goal. It won't matter if users can find the information they need if they end up feeling stupid while trying to do it.

PUT IT TO THE TEST

As we choose the structures we want to use, we should remember that no single perfect structure will fit the needs of every user. Each person's approach to a document, whether online or printed, will be unique.

For example, some users—readers—are strongly inclined to browse a document's or Web site's structure, scanning the table of contents or headings in a printed document or looking for interesting links on a Web page. Other users are more likely to go straight to the index or use the search function to find what they're looking for. Most of us are somewhere in between, selecting a strategy on the basis of our needs at the moment and the visible structure of the document.

In addition to browsing versus searching preferences, countless other factors influence how we use a document. Usability consultant Steve Krug emphasizes this in his book *Don't Make Me Think: A Common Sense Approach to Web Usability* (New Riders Publishing, 2000):

> The more you watch users carefully and listen to them articulate their intentions, motivations, and thought processes, the more you realize that their individual reactions to Web pages are based on so many variables that attempts to describe users in terms of one-dimensional likes and dislikes are futile and counterproductive. Good design, on the other hand, takes this complexity into account.

While Krug is speaking specifically about Web design, the idea can be generalized for print documents as well: There is no "average user."

How do we decide if a design is good, if it is meeting the needs of a wide range of users? Testing. The only way to know whether the structure you have selected works is to watch as a flesh-and-blood reader, someone likely to use your document or Web site, tries to use it. Usability testing doesn't need to be a complicated affair; in fact, Krug says that if you keep it simple, you're more likely to do it. His book provides several guidelines and ideas for what he calls "usability testing on 10 cents a day"; they include the following:

- **Test early.** Create a prototype of your document or Web site and test it with two or three people. This will help you learn whether your basic design choices are on the right track.
- **Test often.** Krug says, "Testing is an iterative process.... You make something, test it, fix it, and test it again."
- **Don't worry about making your test perfect.** Testing isn't supposed to prove or disprove anything; it's supposed to give you input that can help you make design decisions. If you can't recruit a representative sample of your target, recruit a co-worker. Testing with any users—or even just one user—is better than no testing at all.

Whether we're publishing on paper or online, we do our audiences (and, there-fore, ourselves) a favor by taking the time to plan the basic structure of our doc-uments and ways to make data-based searches quick, specific, and fruitful. Think about the advantages to be gained by providing alternative viewpoints to jumpstart an audience's attention, engagement, and comprehension.

The way we organize information is both the means and the end to making it accessible. Good information design is more than a concept; like good design in any medium, it serves the people whose favor it woos.

7

Web Style: Writing, Organizing, Editing

I s the Web a different world? Yes and no. Must we discard all we know and learn to write in a whole new way? No. Are we free to break the shackles of grammar and style, to express ourselves however we choose? No.

Writing for the Web is different from writing for a print publication, but the factors that matter most are *who* the readers are and *how* they will interact with the medium. Writers have been taking those factors into consideration since they first set quill to papyrus.

The people we call Web *users* are, when all is said and done, *readers*. Thus, you may have heard it said that writing, organizing, and editing Web content (and other electronic content read onscreen) is no different from writing, organizing, and editing for print. Good writing is good writing, in any medium! Well, yes and no.

Web content isn't just a plugged-in version of regular old writing-for-the-page. Web style integrates content and presentation in ways directly pegged to the capabilities of online information search, navigation, linking, and sharing—four fundamental capabilities unmatched by even the most carefully planned and executed print publications.

Here's what Patrick Lynch and Sarah Horton say about Web style in their lucid, comprehensive Web Style Guide (webstyleguide.com):

> We seek clarity, order, and trustworthiness in information sources, whether traditional paper documents or Web pages. Effective page design can provide this confidence.... Visual and functional continuity in your Web site organization, graphic design, and typography are essential to convincing your audience that your Web site offers them timely, accurate, and useful information. A careful, systematic approach to page design can simplify navigation, reduce user errors, and make it easier for readers to take advantage of the information and features of the site.

We're in complete agreement that site usability and functionality matter tremendously; in fact, in this section, *organizing* means applying these attributes of online content proactively on behalf of the typical intended reader:

- **Accessibility**—"I can find what I'm looking for."
- **Orientation**—"I understand where I am in the hierarchy of a site or a document."
- **Navigation**—"I know how to go forward and back from a starting point and return from cross-linked information."
- **Interactivity**—"I have a say in how I access and gather the information I need."
- **Readability**—"I can assimilate facts and data easily because heads, subheads, captions, and bulleted lists allow me to skim incrementally through content."
- **Utility**—"I can immediately see the relevance or irrelevance of this content to my needs, which helps me winnow my options." (It's equally "useful" to Web users knowing which sources to skip and which to focus on.)

A perfect example of well-organized Web text that maximizes those attributes is shown on the facing page.

IN A PERFECT WORLD...

Let's pretend that we live in an ideal world. There, if we knew that printed information is also destined for the Web, instead of re-editing it after the fact, we would take into account from the very beginning what current research tells us about the act of reading online.

In a nutshell, writing and editing effectively for the Web require us to make different assumptions about readers, and about the act of reading. To that end, we recommend that you consult the excellent "Editorial Style" discussion in the Lynch-Horton Web Style Guide (webstyleguide.com/style/online-style.html) and subscribe to Jakob Nielsen's free AlertBox newsletters (sign up at useit.com).

For example, from Lynch-Horton's first-rate, nuanced summary of "online style":

> For most Web writing you should assume that your carefully crafted prose will not be read word by word. This is not the case, of course, for texts such as journal articles or teaching materials: In many cases, these more complicated texts will be printed out and read offline. But most online information is best presented using short segments of text written in a clear, concise style and with ample use of editorial landmarks.

HTML TECHNIQUES FOR WEB CONTENT ACCESSIBILITY GUIDELINES 1.0:
W3C NOTE 6, NOVEMBER 2000

This version: http://www.w3.org/TR/2000/NOTE-WCAG10-HTML-TECHS-20001106/
(plain text, PostScript, PDF, gzip tar file of HTML, zip archive of HTML)
Latest version: http://www.w3.org/TR/WCAG10-HTML-TECHS/
Previous version: http://www.w3.org/TR/2000/NOTE-WCAG10-HTML-TECHS-20000920/
Editors:
Wendy Chisholm, W3C;
Gregg Vanderheiden, Trace R & D Center University of Wisconsin—Madison;
Ian Jacobs, W3C
Copyright ©1999–2000 W3C® (MIT, INRIA, Keio), All Rights Reserved. W3C liability, trademark, document use and software licensing rules apply.

Abstract
This document describes techniques for authoring accessible Hypertext Markup Language (HTML) content (refer to HTML 4.01 [HTML4]). This document is intended to help authors of Web content who wish to claim conformance to "Web Content Accessibility Guidelines 1.0" ([WCAG10]). While the techniques in this document should help people author HTML that conforms to "Web Content Accessibility Guidelines 1.0", these techniques are neither guarantees of conformance nor the only way an author might produce conforming content.

This document is part of a series of documents about techniques for authoring accessible Web content. For information about the other documents in the series, please refer to "Techniques for Web Content Accessibility Guidelines 1.0" [WCAG10-TECHS].

Note: This document contains a number of examples that illustrate accessible solutions in CSS but also deprecated examples that illustrate what content developers should not do. The deprecated examples are highlighted and readers should approach them with caution—they are meant for illustrative purposes only.

Status of this document
This version has been published to correct some broken links in the previous version.

The 6 November 2000 version of this document is a Note in a series of Notes produced and endorsed by the Web Content Accessibility Guidelines Working Group (WCAG WG). This Note has not been reviewed or endorsed by W3C Members. The series of documents supersedes the single document 5 May 1999 W3C Note "Techniques for Web Content Accessibility Guidelines 1.0". The topics from the earlier document have been separated into technology-specific documents that may evolve independently. Smaller technology-specific documents allow authors to focus on a particular technology.

While the "Web Content Accessibility Guidelines 1.0" Recommendation [WCAG10] is a stable document, this series of companion documents is expected to evolve as technologies change and content developers discover more effective techniques for designing accessible Web content.

The history of changes to the series of documents as well as the list of open and closed issues are available. Readers are encouraged to comment on the document and propose resolutions to current issues. Please send detailed comments on this document to the Working Group at w3c-wai-gl@w3.org; public archives are available.

The English version of this specification is the only normative version. Translations of this document may be available.

The list of known errors in this document is available at "Errata in Web Content Accessibility Guidelines". Please report errors in this document to wai-wcag-editor@w3.org.

The Web Accessibility Initiative (WAI) of the World Wide Web Consortium (W3C) makes available a variety of resources on Web accessibility. WAI Accessibility Guidelines are produced as part of the WAI Technical Activity. The goals of the Web Content Accessibility Guidelines Working Group are described in the charter.

A list of current W3C Recommendations and other technical documents is available.

We suggest that such guidance works just as well for many kinds of printed texts—a beneficial influence of the Web on communication generally. Conversely, in the mechanical sense of the word *style*, there's no reason to deviate from your print standards: If you follow AP style in your print publications, follow it in your Web publications. There is no universal Web style, just as there is no universal print style.

But some core editorial conventions are accepted by first-rate Web publishers—and they matter more than ever, as the sheer range and quality of publications available online increases:

- **Be concise.** A widely accepted statistic is that people read 25 percent more slowly on a computer screen than on paper. The corollary is that a document written for the Web should be 25 to 50 percent shorter than one written for print—roughly, not literally. Web content should be no longer than—but as long as—it needs to be in order to say what it has to say.
- **Chunk copy.** Use short paragraphs, lots of subheads, and displayed lists for a series of three or more items, if they require emphasis or if each item is more than a few words long. It's not as comfortable to read text on a computer screen, and it's difficult to distinguish certain punctuation marks, such as commas and colons, onscreen. Think in terms of about 1,000 words per screen. Each chunk should be somewhat self-contained, with links connecting it to the other chunks of the document. If you're accustomed to outlining before you write, you may want to sketch how each chunk of your document relates to the others.
- **Write strong prose.** Online readers can become distracted. Not just brevity but fresh, lively writing and accurate delivery of information are requisites for "sticky" online content that engages their attention.
- **Think globally.** Remember that most of the world uses the metric system. When providing US measurements for distance, speed, etc., also include (alongside, in parentheses) the metric equivalent. (Check your dictionary for a conversion chart.) Avoid using the # symbol to indicate pounds; a single quote to indicate feet; and double quotes to indicate inches. These marks aren't recognized everywhere outside the United States. Also avoid metaphors, puns, shorthand, and date-time conventions that won't make sense outside American English and mainstream US culture.

A bit of conventional wisdom is that Web writing is more personal and less formal than print writing. The best writing seems to speak directly to the individual reader, even if, in fact, those readers number in the millions. As for being less formal, it's true that the first and second person are widely accepted online; it's not true that errors of spelling or grammar are okay on the Web. In fact, since readers of Web pages may have little information about the publisher, such errors can detract seriously from a document's credibility: "If these people can't even check their spelling, how likely are they to check their facts?" Speaking of credibility....

E-MAIL COUNTS AS "PUBLISHING"

The creators of ARPANET messaging, a precursor to Internet e-mail, published a paper in 1978 in which they approved of how "one could write tersely and type imperfectly, even to an older person in a superior position and even to a person one did not know very well, and the recipient took no offense."

As for one of the most interactive and prevalent aspects of our publishing lives—e-mail—there's still debate about how much typos and poor grammar matter in e-mail messages.

Many of the Web's founders, themselves articulate standard-bearers for civilized communication, nevertheless accept that e-mail is created so quickly it is liable to formal errors. The Jargon File's own Eric Raymond, replied graciously to the editor of *The Editorial Eye*, who had apologized for a typo in a note she had sent him: "I never take offense at mistypings in e-mail. I don't take offense because as long as I know what you mean I don't even really see the errors."

Likewise, David Crystal, author of the *Cambridge Encyclopedia of the English Language*, says he expects anyone who spots a typo in one of his e-mails to think "Crystal must have typed this in a hurry"—not "Crystal doesn't know what he's talking about."

And it's true that e-mail is a communication tool, not a literary genre. It has conventions, just as other forms of communication do. How you write e-mail depends largely on context. If the only e-mails you send are to your children at college, you don't need to read this section. But if you send business e-mails as well, take another look at what the recipient may be expecting.

- **Use the subject field.** Most e-mail systems display the sender's name and the subject field before the reader actually opens the message. Try to make your subject field as informative as possible, so a reader faced with a dozen e-mails first thing in the morning will have some idea which to open first.
- **Keep it brief.** People are receiving more e-mails every day. Opening and reading one message may take less than a minute, but the minutes add up fast. There's no need to be telegraphic—you're not being charged by the word, after all—but do respect your reader's time. E-mails are like the interoffice memos of yore. Each should address a single topic, and do so succinctly and clearly.
- **Skip most emoticons.** Smiley faces, winks: Some folks claim that readers won't know what's facetious unless they have the cue of an emoticon. For

centuries, though, writers have been able to convey humor perfectly well using words alone. If you doubt your ability to do so, dispense with the attempt at humor (not a bad idea in business communications).

- **Include a formal signature.** You can automate a variety of signatures for different occasions, so there's really no excuse for making people look up your full name and contact information—unless you're writing a very personal note (not a good idea on your office computer).

- **Wait a second.** Once you hit "send," that e-mail is gone beyond recall. Before you send it, take a moment to read through it. Is everything spelled correctly? Have you covered your subject clearly? Most important, have you said anything you'll regret? And check the address box! It's easy to click on an address one line above or below the one you're aiming for, and the consequences can range from embarrassing to horrifying. Or you can accidentally reply to an electronic mailing list posting by a friend of yours and end up posting to the entire list—perhaps slamming other list members in public. The ouch really stings.

Web design is relatively easy to get right, once the publishing goals have been identified—and there are many courses and online resources to assist the willing learner (see the appendix for a selection). But editing content for effective organization, with embedded links, selective emphasis, logical segmentation, and a clear focus—that's a relatively complex undertaking. We've never seen it explained in any detail in any Web writing guide. That's why we're doing it.

A FOUR-STEP PRINT-TO-WEB EDITING TUTORIAL

(**Note:** Visit sciencesitescom.com for the online version from which this material has been adapted, with the permission of Merry Bruns.)

This section is this primarily an overview of the process of thinking about how to edit Web content from the point of view of its intended audience—and that includes an expansion of the definition of *editing*. As a preface to a systematic, field-tested tutorial for migrating print content to the Web, consider what Dorian Benkoil, editorial director of mediabistro.com, wrote in February 2007:

> At the recent Digital Magazine News conference, I thought Endgadget blog chief Peter Rojas might step off the stage and punch a magazine exec who was asserting that readers couldn't trust blogs because they're unreliable. But blogging is no more one single thing than TV or radio or magazines are.

No more than the countless sites that make up the Web are one single thing! Web writing isn't a monolithic activity—any more than writing for print is.

Given that fact, this overview can't do justice to every possible permutation of online style. So, by popular demand, we're offering a focused, step-by-step demystification of Web style in a specific context. Merry Bruns, a seasoned trainer, shares her patented solution for one of the most challenging aspects of Web publishing in most organizations: how to edit printed content for online access.

The repurposing exercises shed light on the core elements of Web style. Keep in mind the big-picture strategies underlying the details of editing for quick Web access:

- Preserve the meaning while more closely focusing the original text.
- Minimize screen-reading eyestrain with screen-friendly formatting.
- Add value to the original text with judicious use of online-only capabilities.
- Build back in useful, optional detail in the form of links, references, graphics, glossaries, etc.

Let's put those strategies into practical context. Ever seen an exploded diagram of a car engine's parts? Separating out the engine parts visually makes it easier to grasp the underlying mechanics and learn how to disassemble all or some of the engine and put it back together. That's one way to think of how to edit printed documents for a Web site: Web publishing offers editors infinite room to take advantage of "exploded" structure, which in turn gives readers infinite possibilities for exploring and assembling information.

Printed material can certainly be migrated successfully. In fact, it's possible to present complex information from various sources more accessibly to readers on the Web than in print. Yet despite its vaunted informality and flexibility, the Web contains thousands of dense, lengthy documents—difficult enough to absorb in printed format—whose publishers haven't adapted printed material at all for Web publication. Plain and simple, that's a mistake.

The term *Web editing* means rearranging material for greater clarity, rewriting parts in a more suitable style, deciding on the best technical presentation, and supplying new material as needed. In the print world, these roles are often very separate—not so if you're a Web editor. Here's what Web editing entails.

1. Know All You Can About All Your Readers

Knowing who the readers are and what they need are the most important things to keep in mind as you begin the Web editing process. And please note the plural form *readers*: Even the most narrowly focused public site has several kinds of potential visitors.

You might think you know who they are already or have a general sense of your core audience. But that's not good enough. It's best to step back and analyze any data, anecdotal or otherwise, that you can get your hands on about everybody who is looking at the site, why they're looking at it, what they expect to find there, and how you can help different readers with different needs—and the same readers with different needs over time. The fact is that most sites have several subaudiences besides a core audience.

If a site is primarily commercial, your focus will be almost entirely on driving readers to learn about (and get excited about) your services—but you may need content for a loyalty program as well as for first-time-buyer incentives. If you're an association or other membership organization, your site should serve its stakeholders first, then potentially draw in new members— oh, and what about a press room for the media? Education sites have attracting new students and serving current students and alumni as equally important goals—but also usually want to showcase community involvement and national and international achievements of professors, and promote corporate partnerships. For starters.

At the macro level, though, most of us basically have three audience types: the known audience, the unknown (and potentially global) visiting audience, and the potential audience you are not yet reaching. How do you find out more about them?

Start by listing what *you* come to a Web site for. What features and characteristics make it a favorite or turn you off? Chances are, you prefer a site with content that is immediately accessible, relevant to your interests and goals, and written in conversational, clear language.

By doing this simple exercise, you can learn a great deal about the subtle, emotional, even illogical reasons people choose one site over another:

- List the three sites, in widely competitive markets, that you enjoy using most often—say, your favorite travel site, bookselling site, and reference site.
- List the reasons that make each of these sites outstanding in their niches.
- Now list three comparable sites in the same markets that you don't choose to regularly visit—you may have to do an online search for competitors, precisely because they don't come to mind if you don't use them! List reasons that make each of the rejects less appealing that your three favorites.

You may want to try a variation of this exercise periodically by surveying some of your own site's readers via e-mail or a small focus group. The ability to second-guess answers to such questions with a fair degree of confidence comes from practicing comparative, critical thinking. We may call people *users*, but their behaviors and loyalties are less mechanical and more unpredictable than we like to think.

Demo: Showing You Know Your Audience
AARP (aarp.org/learntech/computers)

AARP knows its readers well and knows that the over-fifty crowd is getting online in massive numbers.

With their kids to keep them up to date, and more retirement time for activism and education, AARP members often appreciate help, but they don't need their hands held. The Computers and Technology content reflects this understanding while also supporting the corporate mission to advocate for seniors, and that's just good business.

The focus of the articles is on what benefits the AARP member most, and that's not merely the organization's news about itself. Topics are timely, and useful for just about anyone (kids included). Sample topics like these:

2. Restructure the Information
The central goals of restructuring content for the Web are to make the most important information immediately accessible and to subordinate supporting information. The process of meeting those goals begins with breaking a print document into smaller, more editorially manageable chunks.

Later, you'll edit and rewrite all this as necessary—obviously, it'll lack transitions, contextual references, and narrative development. But this is stripping information back to basics. (If you find there's not much of a "there" left underneath a lot of initially lengthy exposition, you've got a different problem. You can't highlight important information if it isn't important to begin with. But it's better to find that out early before posting it for the world to be bored and annoyed by.)

In many cases, "chunking" simply means breaking a well-signposted linear piece down into topics and subtopics. In other cases, though, the process isn't as neat. The task is to pull out *all* the main topics and points that a document contains, no matter where they are, or whatever form they take—statements, examples, evidence, phrases, statistics, graphs.

That's one of the most difficult things for someone new to Web editing: removing transitions, contextual references, and narrative development—the very elements that a print editor strives to strengthen and often supplies. And you will edit back in and rewrite those elements later as needed.

But for now, without any regard for the existing structure, isolate *all* the key blocks of text for reordering to take advantage of the Web as a publishing medium. These may be statements, examples, evidence, phrases, headlines, direct quotes, whole paragraphs—it's all being unformatted so it can stand out as vital information.

Not all print editors would tackle the same printed piece the same way; Web editors develop their own work style, too. Some dive into the electronic files of an original document, copying and pasting key points into a new document as they're identified. Others start by making notes on the original printed version or highlighting statements and paragraphs containing ideas that deserve prominence.

By whatever method, once the informational chunks have been identified and extracted, the task is to reorder them for further editing—making a coherent story following inverted pyramid style, as journalists do. Web readers appreciate a structure that allows them to grasp the main point immediately and decide for themselves how much detail to pursue.

So place the main point/idea/fact first, followed by the rest in descending order of importance. "Descending order of importance" to whom? To your multiple known and potential audiences, of course—whose needs and interests you've had in mind from the beginning. Set aside anything that doesn't directly support any of the main ideas.

3. Format Content for Scanning

It's time to create a hierarchical draft of the revised material from the main message(s) and supporting information you've pulled out; set aside (but do not delete) anything that doesn't directly support the main argument.

At this point, you'll have pages (probably printed-out and well scribbled-on) of content that's about ready to put online. Now it's time to think about laying out text for easy scanning (critical skimming). You need to format it, which means creating a text layout that will make it possible for your readers to skim for the main points and the general direction of the material. If they find something that interests them, perhaps they'll test-drive a bit of supporting information to see whether there's depth here worth attention.

If you've formatted text so people can quickly assess its relevance, even if they leave the site, you've shown respect for their time by not making them invest a lot of it in figuring out what you're up to. That's an equally important function of formatting: allowing people to skip reading before they become disappointed.

The Web editor's two biggest challenges in formatting text for scannability are (1) selecting the presentation that supports quick access and (2) selectively highlighting what's "must-read"—what you want readers to notice, even if that's all they notice.

Start by categorizing the material.　What type of information is it? Steps for changing a tire? Instructions for registering for a conference? Driving directions to a location? If your material is essentially telling people how to perform a task, you can be sure they're not on your site for beautiful prose. Your goal is to help readers meet their goals, get off the page, and move on to the next thing they want to do.

But what if your material consists of feature articles, professional reports, biographies, scholarly documents, or informational articles? Here you don't have to lose the carefully crafted prose style, but give readers clear headers and subheads to help them navigate easily through the material.

- For pragmatic, goal-oriented copy, think numbered points, bulleted lists, short sentences, and very short, boldface form-field and subsection locators. Your goal is to help people complete the task quickly and efficiently and get off the page and on to the next thing they want to do.
- For feature articles, white papers, policy analyses, regulatory briefings, biographies, STM (scholarly, technical, and medical) documents, and many other types of fact-based information, you don't necessarily have to lose the prose style. But you'll need to supply clear heads and subheads to help readers navigate through greater complexity.

Then highlight the can't-miss information.　This is the text you should highlight graphically in some way. Boldface keywords to make them stand out. Tighten paragraphs to turn dense writing into easily digestible chunks. Bullet-list a string of ideas or a list of items. Remember, if you've bulleted or bolded something, you're guaranteeing that the reader will look at it. So make sure these items are worth the special treatment you're giving them.

But used with care, boldfacing will make key terms stand out. And bulleted lists of things will be instantly visible. Heads and subheads will help people recognize an orderly sequence of topics on the page. Keeping paragraphs short is also a way to highlight key information—perhaps even a single crisp, significant sentence. Try to avoid editing all paragraphs down to exactly the same brief word count, though, and giving them all a perfunctory subhead. Even on the Web, text that offers variety in paragraphing is more attractive to the reading eye.

This is almost the only control you're ever going to have over how someone looks at your Web site! You control, with emphatic formatting, where the eye will fall first on site content. Key items will be picked up (because they're bolded). A list of instructions or options will be instantly visible (because they're numbered or bulleted). The hierarchy of related topics will be clear (because you added meaningful headers and subheads).

As you look at the example in the exercise, note what your eyes are doing as you scan the document. What grabs your attention? What do you read first, what are you skipping past? In this exercise, you're practicing your skill at assessing scannability.

Demo: Formatting Text for Scanning

Below is a sample of text I've taken from Jakob Nielsen's Alertbox. I've stripped out all his formatting, so you're seeing only the text itself (not as it was published). Read it through and think about the message: A statement of opinion has been expressed and data is being used to back it up.

Unedited text: Alertbox for October 18, 1998:

Failure of Corporate Websites
On the average, the Web doesn't work: When you think of something to do on the Web, the expected outcome is that you will fail. Some recent data to support this claim. In Jared Spool's study of 15 large commercial sites users could only find information 42% of the time even though they were taken to the correct home page before they were given the test tasks. A study from Zona Research found that 62% of Web shoppers have given up looking for the item they wanted to buy online (and 20% had given up more than three times during a two-month period). Forrester Research audited 20 major sites, finding 51% compliance with simple Web usability principles such as "is the site organized by user goals?" and "does a search list retrievals in order of relevance?" (in other words, the average site violated half of these simple design principles)

Despite these miserable statistics, users do benefit from the Web since they spend most of their time on the good sites. But the odds are against them when they want to try something new. And the odds are against any company that wants to put up a website: in my estimate 90% of commercial websites have poor usability. The recent Forrester report is particularly interesting because it tries to identify the reasons for the many bad corporate websites as well as the impact on a company from having a bad site. Many of Forrester's conclusions are similar to my writings in the Alertbox since 1995 and the report provides additional supportive data from large corporate Web projects.

Problem: Where's the data? You can't differentiate the statistics from the text very easily, as they're all run together.

Solution: Take a look at the original online document. The statistics are bulleted out, some text is bolded, and subheads popped in. What's the thinking behind this? When factual information is buried, and it's statistical to boot, nobody will want to dig for it, or, if they do, the chances are upped that even motivated readers will miss the point. Presenting numbers and statistics in text is a bear, but you can compensate by setting them off as here: by using bullets, bolding the statistics, and providing enough context to allow comprehension on a quick scanning.

Edited Text: Alertbox as it appeared online

useit.com → Alertbox → Oct. 1998 Failure of corporate sites

Jakob Nielsen's Alertbox for October 18, 1998:

Failure of Corporate Websites

On the average, the Web doesn't work: when you think of something to do on the Web, the **expected outcome is that you will fail**. Some recent data to support this claim:

- In Jared Spool's study of 15 large commercial sites users could only **find information 42% of the time** even though they were taken to the correct home page before they were given the test tasks
- A study from Zona Research found that **62% of Web shoppers have given up** looking for the item they wanted to buy online (and 20% had given up more than three times during a two-month period)
- Forrester Research audited 20 major sites, finding **51% compliance with simple Web usability principles** such as "is the site organized by user goals?" and "does a search list retrievals in order of relevance?" (in other words, the average site violated half of these simple design principles)

Despite these miserable statistics, users do benefit from the Web since they spend most of their time on the good sites. But the odds are against them when they want to try something new. And the **odds are against any company that wants to put up a website**: in my estimate 90% of commercial websites have poor usability.

The recent Forrester report is particularly interesting because it tries to identify the reasons for the many bad corporate websites as well as the impact on a company from having a bad site. Many of Forrester's conclusions are similar to my writings in the Alertbox since 1995 and the report provides additional supportive data from large corporate Web projects.

Demo: More Formatting for Easy Scanning

Look at the "Before Editing" example below. If you had to read this online, would you have an easy time figuring out what the author's trying to tell you?

Before Editing

Poultry: Chicken and turkey. Select lean cuts. The leanest poultry choice is white meat from the breast of chicken or turkey, without the skin. Although skinless dark meat is leaner than some cuts of beef or pork, it has nearly twice the fat calories as does white meat. Many grocery stores have both ground chicken and ground turkey. But know that when choosing ground poultry it may have as much fat as ground beef has, or more, because it includes dark meat and skin. To make the leanest choice, choose ground breast meat, or look for low-fat ground chicken or turkey. Buy poultry that feels cold to the touch. Fresh poultry needs to be cold at all times to help prevent bacterial contamination. Make poultry, along with meat and fish, among the last items you put in your shopping cart before checkout. Choose poultry that looks moist and supple. Avoid poultry that has signs of drying, discoloration, blemishes or bruising. Fresh poultry has a mild scent and is free of strong odors. Don't buy poultry past the expiration date. Some poultry packages display a "sell by" or "use before" date. A sell-by date tells stores how long the product should remain on the shelves. A use-before date is the last date you should consume the product, to guarantee the best flavor and quality. Don't buy products past these recommended dates. Use fresh poultry within two days. Store poultry toward the back of your refrigerator, which tends to be the coldest space. Make sure no juices drip from the poultry onto other foods, particularly fresh produce, in the refrigerator. Freeze poultry in store packaging. Leave on the wrapping and add a second layer of airtight, heavy-duty plastic wrap before placing poultry in your freezer. Use frozen poultry sections within nine months and whole poultry within one year. Thaw frozen poultry in the refrigerator before use. Bacteria can grow rapidly on poultry at room temperature. Thawing poultry in the refrigerator, however, can take two or more days, depending on the size of the pieces. Defrosting poultry in the microwave is another option. If you use this method, cook the poultry immediately after defrosting or put the pieces back in the refrigerator if you're marinating it. Also, use the "defrost" or "50-percent power" setting to thaw the poultry so that the edges don't cook while the rest of the meat remains frozen. Avoid contaminating other foods. Use different cutting boards and separate knives when preparing raw poultry. Wash your hands and all of the utensils and surfaces—plates and cutting boards, for example—that come in contact with the raw poultry or its juices before using them with other foods. Cut off the skin and visible fat before cooking poultry. This lowers the fat content, and if you're grilling, helps prevent flare-ups, which can char the meat and form unhealthy compounds. If you're roasting a whole chicken or turkey, remove the skin after cooking, but before you carve and serve the meat. Cook thoroughly before eating. To see if the meat is cooked through to its center, cut into the thickest part. Any juices should run clear. The meat should show no signs of uncooked or pink flesh. If using a food thermometer, check to make sure it registers 165 F for ground poultry, 170 F for breast portions and 180 F for whole birds.

Problem: The author probably knows what the document's about, but he decided to put it online unedited; unfortunately, all his work has pretty much gone to waste. It's highly doubtful that anyone will take the time to figure out, piece by piece, what the writer's talking about.

Solution: What we have to do is analyze the text, and figure out what topics are being discussed in the document. Make a list of all the main thoughts if necessary, and rearrange them in a new hierarchy, if you feel that's necessary, in order of importance. Your goal is to make it easy for the reader to SEE the sections and subjects and scan them quickly, and you'll do this by using formatting techniques. Should main thoughts be titled, or given subheads? How many items are being talked about here, and which ones are the most important?

Now take a look at the formatted version below. Look carefully at what's been done to the individual blocks of text. Can you see the structure clearly now, without much effort? The main topics have been pulled out—labeled, set off in bullets, and their first lines bolded. This makes for an easy skim.

Another important point: Standardize your formatting. Once readers get used to how you're formatting the document, they can scroll down the page, *ignoring* the formatting you've put in, and concentrating on the words. And that's the whole point, isn't it?

After Editing: Text Only
(You can see this online at mayoclinic.com/health/food-and-nutrition/ NU00202/LOCID.)

POULTRY: CHICKEN AND TURKEY

Selecting

- **Select lean cuts.** The leanest poultry choice is white meat from the breast of chicken or turkey, without the skin. Although skinless dark meat is leaner than some cuts of beef or pork, it has nearly twice the fat calories as does white meat. Many grocery stores have both ground chicken and ground turkey. But know that when choosing ground poultry it may have as much fat as ground beef has, or more, because it includes dark meat and skin. To make the leanest choice, choose ground breast meat, or look for low-fat ground chicken or turkey.
- **Buy poultry that feels cold to the touch.** Fresh poultry needs to be cold at all times to help prevent bacterial contamination. Make poultry, along with meat and fish, among the last items you put in your shopping cart before checkout.

- **Choose poultry that looks moist and supple.** Avoid poultry that has signs of drying, discoloration, blemishes, or bruising. Fresh poultry has a mild scent and is free of strong odors.
- **Don't buy poultry past the expiration date.** Some poultry packages display a "sell by" or "use before" date. A sell-by date tells stores how long the product should remain on the shelves. A use-before date is the last date you should consume the product, to guarantee the best flavor and quality. Don't buy products past these recommended dates.

Storing

- **Use fresh poultry within two days.** Store poultry toward the back of your refrigerator, which tends to be the coldest space. Make sure no juices drip from the poultry onto other foods, particularly fresh produce, in the refrigerator.
- **Freeze poultry in store packaging.** Leave on the wrapping and add a second layer of airtight, heavy-duty plastic wrap before placing poultry in your freezer. Use frozen poultry sections within nine months and whole poultry within one year.
- **Thaw frozen poultry in the refrigerator before use.** Bacteria can grow rapidly on poultry at room temperature. Thawing poultry in the refrigerator, however, can take two or more days, depending on the size of the pieces. Defrosting poultry in the microwave is another option. If you use this method, cook the poultry immediately after defrosting or put the pieces back in the refrigerator if you're marinating it. Also, use the "defrost" or "50-percent power" setting to thaw the poultry so that the edges don't cook while the rest of the meat remains frozen.

Cooking

- **Avoid contaminating other foods.** Use different cutting boards and separate knives when preparing raw poultry. Wash your hands and all of the utensils and surfaces—plates and cutting boards, for example—that come in contact with the raw poultry or its juices before using them with other foods.
- **Cut off the skin and visible fat before cooking poultry.** This lowers the fat content, and if you're grilling, helps prevent flare-ups, which can char the meat and form unhealthy compounds. If you're roasting a whole chicken or turkey, remove the skin after cooking, but before you carve and serve the meat.
- **Cook thoroughly before eating.** To see if the meat is cooked through to its center, cut into the thickest part. Any juices should run clear. The meat

should show no signs of uncooked or pink flesh. If using a food thermometer, check to make sure it registers 165 F for ground poultry, 170 F for breast portions and 180 F for whole birds.

4. Tighten Verbose Text

There's no room for verbal clutter online. We absorb messages better in short phrases—think billboards, headlines, pullquotes. But does that mean that all online text needs to be as much as 50 percent shorter that its original printed version? Some writers have said just that. I don't agree. I believe that text well-formatted for quicker reading will do just well in most cases.

What you're trying to do is write more conversationally, more the way people talk to each other face to face. This kind of writing is to the point and also more interesting to listen to. When in doubt about the writing, try reading it out loud. Does it sound like something that would actually come out of anyone's mouth? If it doesn't:

* Look for shorter ways of phrasing overly complex statements. For example, *have a tendency to* can become *tends to*; *the field of science* can become *science.*
* Kill weak, redundant phrases and substitute strong ones: *perform a test* can become *test*; *do a review* can become *review*; *serves to explain* can become *explains.*
* Passive voice and smothered verbs can make for weaker sentences, so try to use action verbs: *was sent a letter of explanation for the delay* can become *received a letter explaining the delay.*

Demo: Tightening Verbose Text

Take a look at this sentence. On paper, it reads like any rather long-winded paragraph, but doesn't give us much trouble. But put online, it becomes somewhat impenetrable, adding to its woes:

Before Editing

In spite of the fact that the educational environment is a very unique and significant facet to each and every one of our children in terms of his or her future development, some groups do not support reasonable and fair tax assessments that are required for providing an educational experience at a high level of quality.

Problem: As we scan text, overly verbose writing styles like this act as a road-block to understanding. The reader spends more time trying to figure out what on earth's being said than paying attention to what is means.

Solution: Now look at the series of possible edits. As we cut back wordy text to only the words that matter most, we're reducing it to its essence. *In spite of the fact that* becomes *although*. *Each and every one of our children in terms of his or her future development* becomes *our children's development*. You get the idea. We're trying to "re-say" the text using far fewer words, with the challenge of not losing meaning along the way. By Edit 3, the focus has also shifted. You may or may not want that, but trying different edits will help you find one that says it all.

After three possible editing passes
Edit 1. Although the educational environment is a unique and significant part of our children's development, some groups oppose the reasonable, fair tax assessments required for a quality education.

Edit 2. Although the educational environment is a uniquely significant part of our children's development, some groups oppose the reasonable tax assessments that provide it.

Edit 3. Some groups oppose reasonable tax assessments that can provide a high-quality education for our children.

Demo: Writing Pointers, Not Prose

Not all online text has to be written in sentence or paragraph form. Sometimes an outline—a map—built from short phrases pointing to the reader's navigational or search options is just the ticket. Ask two questions about content to decide whether it may be better formatted that way:

- **Is it strictly navigational?** Keep the writing brief—even telegraphic. Readers are trying to get to a specific page or kind of information. It isn't rude to point online.
- **Is it strictly instructional?** Keep the writing brief but completely clear and complete enough to accomplish an objective. People aren't there for a narrative excursion—they want to know how to apply for a job or order a book.

GEICO's homepage, geico.com/home, is short and sweet. Homeowners are presumably motivated to find specific policy-related information. Once *there*, they'll settle in and read. But they don't want to do that while they're still in action mode, discovering all the options; the same thing we do with sample topics like these:

WHEN YOU'RE NOT ALLOWED TO EDIT

The things we've talked about in this section can pertain both to long articles as well as shorter ones. A lengthy document placed unedited online (say, as a PDF) has a double problem: It's both physically and psychologically daunting to the reader, offering no navigation relief. It must be read one static screenful at a time.

The formatting techniques discussed can aid both the skimming and careful reading experience tremendously. For a very long document that you're not allowed to edit in any significant way, you can at least write a brief summary statement, editorial lead, or abstract telling the reader what the document's about: "Five ways to manage your diabetes, with detailed information for children, adults, and seniors" is a lot more informative than starting out cold with a long scroll of dense unbroken text. You'll at least alert the reader to what the document (in all its unedited lengthiness) is about, giving them the option of printing it out for digesting later or chewing through it online.

The fours steps for editing Web content are adaptable, depending on your publishing mission and the nature of your content.

MYTHS ABOUT WRITING FOR "WEB READERS"

Mick Doherty, former managing editor of the Jetnet, the employee portal of American Airlines, American Eagle, and TWA, once stated the First Rule of Online Publishing this way: "For the first time in the history of the written word, authors, editors, and publishers no longer control the user-end interface." The material in this section is excerpted from articles published in *The Editorial Eye.*

Since 1991, when Tim Berners-Lee first proposed a "World Wide Web project" on Usenet, the laundry list of obstacles to universal Web publishing standards has grown:

- Multiple computer platforms
- Competing Web browsers with multiple versions
- Increase in nonstandard information interfaces (wireless handhelds, telephones)
- Increased user personalization of settings and filtering of content
- Increase in number of plug-ins required and available
- Internet Service Provider (ISP) issues

Web publishing pioneer John December addressed many of these challenges as long ago in the November 2000 issue of *The Editorial Eye.* He politely stated the problem: "An online publication does not necessarily offer the uniform reading experience that paper publications can achieve."

The sudden, sinking realization that Web publishing wrests some presentational control away from wordsmiths and managing editors has caused grave consternation (read: fear) among professional communicators throughout the Web's first decade-plus. Three commonly held but mistaken assumptions make life harder than it has to be for writers, and these myths need correcting.

Myth 1: Web Writers Should Learn How to Design

The lack of ability to uniformly control how Web content is presented to an audience has caused hiring managers to look for writers who can design (and the reverse) and has driven far too many writers to spend hours learning software programs and tweaking HTML code until it's just...exactly... right...wait...not yet...now!

While this might sound counterintuitive, Doherty has said, "That loss of control can be incredibly *empowering* to wordsmiths and editors if they don't waste hours trying to essentially change professions."

Only one visual element of an online presentation can be predetermined: the *words.* As online copywriting guru Nick Usborne has put it, "Words don't care which browser your [readers] use."

Of course, the text and images of any message, in any medium, should be complementary. But on the Web, where the interface your readers will see is simply a best guess, the words must also be strong enough to *stand alone* to deliver the message independently of design—a mandate that does not apply to print.

If the graphics team you work with "gets it," they'll understand that concept. And if they don't, ask them to log on to the site with you and then point out to them that while their typically excellent and engaging graphics are loading, it's quite likely that visitors to the site will begin reading the text without them, as text inevitably loads first.

Put more forcefully, designers live by the axiom that you never get a second chance to make a first impression. So remind them that the typical download process guarantees that in the beginning, the first impression is based entirely on the *words*. Ergo, text—language—matters online.

Let's imagine that you're publishing to a specific, predefined audience—for instance, an employee intranet using company-issued PCs with preloaded browsers inside a firewall on a high-speed connection—and that you're confident about the accuracy of the Photoshop blueline (yep, it's still called that in some shops) the design group develops. But what if that's the day the CEO buys a wireless handheld and tries to load today's headlines from an RSS feed? What's the primary information currency of the PDA? *Words.* That's a lesson not just for writers but for everyone evaluating the importance of good writing online.

Myth 2: All "Web Readers" Are Alike

The popular concept of a homogeneous audience known as "Web readers" is as patently ridiculous as lumping together all "book readers." Unfortunately, this misconception was compounded by early Web publishers, who not only discussed the tendencies of "all *Web readers*" but also stressed that online publishing was available to "*all* Web readers."

Books have always been available to anyone who wanted them, in libraries and bookstores, but no reasonable author ever studied "the tendencies of book readers" to learn how to make a work in progress appealing to "anyone" with "book access."

No, the concept of targeting a specific audience has always been the driving force behind professional writing, and concerns about the visual limitations of a medium should not overshadow the importance of the message. Nothing about the Web changes the fact that writers need to write to the audience they want to reach. In fact, it's more important than ever.

What's the reason that writing for a predefined audience is more important? "All Web readers" do have *one* thing in common: They are, to use the parlance of human-computer interaction (HCI) professionals, also *users.* This redefinition of readers as *users* represents a very real shift in boundaries between publishers and audience.

Karen McGrane, senior director of information architecture with Razorfish, has described this sea change: "When writing is published to the Web, the reader's activity becomes *interactivity.* Awareness that the reader of a document on the Web is also the user of a computer system should make writers more aware of the...activities that users must engage in to meet their goals."

Interactivity between writers and readers isn't new, of course. However, the immediacy of the interaction and the ability of the reader to alter the presentation of the message—and, increasingly, to participate in writing and editing the message—furthers the original point: The one part of a Web site that "users" can't alter is the *words*.

That's why carefully defining the intended audience for online copy is even more important than it has always been in print.

Myth 3: There Is Only One "Web Style"

Widely acknowledged usability expert Jakob Nielsen caused significant trouble for copywriters everywhere when he announced that on the Web, authors should "write no more than 50 percent of the text you would have used in a hardcopy publication." Of course, that's preposterous. If a writer can cut the message by half without affecting the content, the copy was too long in the first place.

The answer isn't to divide the Web version into shorter paragraphs and fewer pages; Nielsen himself consistently argues that a certain percentage of readers are lost with each added click deeper into a site's structure. And yet the litany of "rules for good Web writing" persists: Use lots of bulleted lists and subheads. Keep it short. Take advantage of the ability to link. Keep it short. Write using the "inverted pyramid" of newspaper style. Keep it short. Make sure the writing integrates with the site design. Did we mention that you should keep it short?

Publications have style guides. The Web is not a publication but a media outlet for every conceivable type of publication. Therefore, the Web has room for—and in fact *requires*—many different types of style guides. Many types of writers.

There's nothing magic about "writing short" if the topic warrants more depth or if the presentation is better as one longer, scrolling page rather than several interlinked nodes. Your audience's expectations, preferences, and experience should be the driving force in any decision about online copy presentation.

WHAT TO DO? WRITE FOR *YOUR* AUDIENCE

Technology allows you to gather once unimaginably precise demographics about who is reading your online publication, but that same technology has taken away the security blanket of fixed format. Breathe deeply and remember these Web writing guidelines:

- You can't control how the publication will actually look to your readers, but you *can* control the quality of the written content, which is what they see first.
- You need to recognize your audience as "users" with the ability to individually change the look and feel of what they are reading; this allows you to focus on them as "readers."
- You can stop trying to follow a monolithic "Web style," much less trying to write for a single, all-encompassing "Web audience," and develop a style that fits the needs and expectations of your specific audience.

The main ideas here apply to all electronic interfaces, including e-mail. The proliferation of widely varying e-mail clients, the increasing popularity of Web-based e-mail, and ongoing arguments regarding the virtues of HTML e-mail versus text-only e-mail all spring from the same seed: Final interface control belongs to the user.

In the end, this technology-enabled shift in control over the publication medium leads back to and reinforces the oldest of all writing maxims: Know your audience. Write to that *specific* audience in ways they will recognize and appreciate, whether or not those ways fit within anybody's prescriptive "best practices" for Web writing. It's no longer possible to know what your audience will see, so you'd better nail what they're going to *read*.

"MULTIMODALITY": MAKING THE WEB ACCESSIBLE FOR ALL

As increasing numbers of print periodicals launch online editions, and as ever more Web sites clamor for original content, editors and designers are encountering a challenging new issue—how to make sure Web content is accessible to people with disabilities.

Nearly 20 percent of the population has some disability—visual, auditory, physical, cognitive, or neurological—that requires them to seek assistance when trying to use online information. Initiatives to better serve this significant portion of the population are being actively pursued by public, private, and nonprofit sectors.

According to the World Wide Web Consortium (W3C), an international organization dedicated to establishing universal Web accessibility through cooperative standards, typical site designs are littered with obstacles like these for disabled users:

- Uncaptioned graphics, video, and audio
- Poorly marked-up tables or frames
- Lack of keyboard options
- Incompatibility with screen-reading programs
- Lack of visual signposts in text
- Overly complex presentation or language
- Flickering or strobing visual elements

To remove these and other barriers to access, the W3C (w3.org) has developed guidelines that have become models for governments and organizations worldwide. They are collectively called the Web Accessibility Initiative and cover Web technologies and protocols, software, and Web content.

Of special interest to editors and designers are the Web Content Accessibility Guidelines (w3.org/TR/WCAG20). The model for groundbreaking legislation in the United States, these guidelines have become the de facto industry standard.

Section 508: Providing Access to the Government

Section 508 of the Federal Rehabilitation Act, issued in December 2000, requires federal agencies to ensure that all electronic and information technology developed or installed after June 21, 2001, is accessible to disabled employees and private citizens. This applies to software packages, databases, photocopiers, telephones, even desktop and laptop computers—and agency Web sites.

Among other things, Section 508 requires that Web pages incorporate text equivalents for nontext items, identifiers for table elements, and alternatives to multimedia presentations. The regulations also provide guidance on style sheets, image maps, scripts, and forms. With few exceptions, the language of Section 508 hews closely to that of the W3C guidelines. "When possible, we tried to adopt their concept if not their language," says Doug Wakefield, the Section 508 point man for the Access Board, the independent federal agency responsible for drafting the regulation. But there is an important difference between the two. "The W3C recommendations were written as guidelines," says Wakefield. "Ours are enforceable standards."

What about the effort required to make Web sites compliant? "The implications are not as stark as they may seem," he says. Existing pages can be left as they are unless their content is modified after Section 508 takes effect. Wakefield cites a recent study estimating that federal agencies operate approximately 20,000 Web sites totaling 35 million Web pages. "You can't realistically expect all these pages to be made compliant, any more than you could order the Empire State Building to be rebuilt with accessibility features."

Nevertheless, webmasters are concerned that even the task of creating new pages according to the Section 508 standard will be inordinately labor-intensive. Not all Web-based authoring software has options for incorporating accessibility, although some software can validate that Web site code meets WAI standards.

"Those of us on the front lines who are churning out pages daily, we *want* to do this," says Mary Jo Lazun, a webmaster for the Treasury Department's Financial Management Service. "But our vast amount of tabular financial data presents problems." Comprehending this type of information and its correlations is tightly tied to a visual presentation: Data in a fixed format such as a table can't be easily "read" independently of that format by alternative means.

Many federal webmasters face similar difficulties in presenting the complex information produced by their agencies in a format that's easy to use. Regarding her own site's preparedness, Lazun says, "Right now we are as compliant as possible within the constraints of software and manpower. We may just have to wait until our tools get better."

Multimodality for the "Functionally Disabled" Too

It appears that webmasters like Lazun will not have to wait long. Mike Paciello, founder and chief technology officer of WebAble, Inc., a provider of accessibility technologies and services, believes the computer industry is taking accessibility into serious consideration. Paciello, who helped draft both the W3C guidelines and the federal regulations, says, "Once people are made aware of the need, the issues, and the strategies for solutions, they almost always respond." Assistive technologies, it is predicted, will flourish when the industry agrees on consistent standards.

And the benefits of assistive technologies extend beyond the disability community. The same features that allow Web pages to be accessible to screen readers and Braille-output-devices also enable them to be displayed on personal data assistants (PDAs), cellular phones, Internet kiosks, and WebTV.

Adobe offers a PDF version that incorporates accessibility features such as support for screen readers, more highly contrasting colors, and keyboard shortcuts. A tagging feature allows screen-reading software to interpret formatting features such as columns, tables, and hyperlinks.

To incorporate this capability, called *multimodality*, Web editors should examine a page the way a person with a disability would. Pretend you don't see, don't hear, and can't move. Determine whether a graphic can be rendered in speech. With streaming media, turn down the volume, and think about what it would mean to a person who is deaf. Think about how a person with no arms would interact with it. Over time, the things that ensure accessibility will come naturally.

One of the hardest things for designers to overcome is the temptation to fixate on how it looks. But if designers will use structural tags rather than formatting tags, most screen readers can better "hear" the former. In style sheets, instead of defining fixed measurements, set adjustable proportions such as percentages that can be redefined as need be by users. Writing with accessibility in mind makes a much more usable site for everyone.

Productivity and comfort matter as much as simple accessibility to basic information. Thus, the definition of *disability* is being broadened to include *functional disability*. Web editors have to take into account people who are "disabled" by multitasking—doing more than one task at a time with incomplete focus on either. Global positioning systems are an example of information rendered multimodal; graphic map information has become voice-activated text.

Is the Web a Public Service?

One of the farthest-reaching potential effects of this shift is the tendency to define the Web as a public accommodation, like a bookstore or a movie theater. If the Web is in fact designated a public service—as the government is being urged by some to do—it will fall under the purview of that other landmark piece of disability legislation, the Americans with Disabilities Act (ADA). Advocates such as the American Foundation for the Blind have given congressional testimony that that ADA should apply to the Web. A landmark 1996 opinion letter issued by the Department of Justice stated that Web sites of organizations covered by ADA should be subject to the Act's accessibility requirements. The issue is contentious but remains untested.

The community of Web users is growing in both number and diversity and challenging online publishing standards. Content guidelines and assistive technologies developed for people with disabilities allow Web site content to reach a wider audience, but Web editors and designers have to reconsider the traditional relationship between content and presentation. Whether enforced voluntarily or through legislation, the universally accessible Web is coming.

8

The Rules Used to Matter.
What Now?

EI Press editors take a consensus approach to style and usage. That means we derive the rationales for our decisionmaking (including to spell *decisionmaking* solid) from a number of authoritative contemporary sources. One of them is us.

EEI Press editors wrote a major style guide (*The New York Public Library Writer's Guide to Style and Usage,* for HarperCollins) and each month we publish our widely admired (if we do say so ourselves) subscription newsletter, *The Editorial Eye* (and have been doing so since 1978). We've edited, written, and critiqued, hundreds of client publications—and created style guides for them.

We regularly consult major style guides, and we teach editorial seminars for which we do research on style and usage. We hear about the thorniest issues confronting our students, and our colleagues on publishing discussion lists pool educated guesses and linguistic citations. And by the way, we love doing all of this.

That's not to say we have all the answers, but one thing we know for certain: Among professional communicators, the drive toward error-free, clear, compelling content is as intense as it ever was—and that goes for online and offline content.

Please quote us if you're trying to make the business case to start or maintain a formal quality control process at your shop: The quality of content has never mattered more, in every medium. That means we have to make good decisions about writing. But we can't deny the energy that Internet publishing has brought to traditional editorial gatekeeping, which has been characterized, not to put too fine a point on it, as, uh, well, dead.

WHAT STYLE AND USAGE ARE FOR
Style decisions are usually based on exemplary guidelines published by large organizations that do a lot of publishing. Style is not based on the same universally

agreed-on set of rules that grammar is. Essentially mechanical in nature, most style decisions are, to put it bluntly, followed "just because."

A working definition of style is "a customary manner of presenting printed material, including usage, punctuation, spelling, typography, and arrangement." Carefully, consistently applied style goes a long way toward fruitful, clean prose that does its work in a particular context.

That's all style is for. Not to worry editors (or give them a truncheon to wield). It's really for readers. And it works by not getting in the way. And the not-getting-in-the-way happens when we follow the accepted practices of a major style guide.

But nobody follows all the rules in any one style guide. Another definition of style is "the fashion of the moment," and editorial and design conventions do change over time to reflect what's going on in wider publishing circles, as well as advances in a specific niche, industry, or professional discipline.

When you have the chance to make a style decision, welcome it! It's an opportunity to create order. Here are a couple things to bear in mind:

- Your choice should reflect the existing personal or corporate style you have been using up until now—if you have one. If you have a more conservative style with a tendency to capitalize words and hyphenate prefixes and unit modifiers, you'll probably choose to write *e-mail* rather than *email.*
- The tendency in English (to which there are many exceptions, naturally) is for terms to go from two words (*cyber café*) to a hyphenated term (*cyber-café*) to one word (*cybercafé*). Where you decide to come down on this continuum is likewise a factor of your existing style, as well as how familiar the term is likely to be to your readers. It's also a good idea to look around and see how the rest of the world is treating the word (although you won't find complete agreement, or you wouldn't have to be making a decision in the first place).

If you're trying to style a term your own organization or profession has added to the lexicon—for which you can find no precedent—ask the smartest editor you know in your field what makes most sense. Or check with one of the resources in the appendix, or Google your wayward term to learn how other editors and publications in your field are handling it.

Usage simply means the way we've agreed to define words the same way and follow the conventions of standard American English so we can understand each other. Usage decisions should be made as consistently as possible and in keeping with conventionally accepted practice, as shown in the newest editions of major dictionaries and usage guides—but, increasingly, that's easier said than done.

The information revolution is essentially a change in the speed of communication—and sped-up communication affects just about every field of human endeavor. The jargon of technology, and of specialized disciplines aided by it, is entering the mainstream—adapted for nontechnical contexts by low-tech types and, sometimes, seeded with humorous subtexts by the digerati.

A good example is the verb *spam*, which has crossed over from the hacker's lexicon into mainstream English. Originally, the verb meant "to crash a program by inputting excessive amounts of data." It now generally refers to unsolicited, mass-mailed, unwanted e-mail or newsgroup postings. As a noun, *spam* refers to the actual message or messages—Internet junk mail.

SPAM, of course, is the registered trademark of Hormel Foods Corporation. We found the following bit of advice on the spam.com Web site, which is owned by Hormel Foods:

> Use of the term SPAM was adopted as a result of the Monty Python skit in which a group of Vikings sang a chorus of "SPAM, SPAM, SPAM..." in an increasing crescendo, drowning out other conversation. Hence, the analogy applied because UCE (unsolicited commercial e-mail) was drowning out normal discourse on the Internet.
>
> We do not object to use of this slang term to describe UCE, although we do object to the use of our product image in association with that term. Also, if the term is to be used, it should be used in all lowercase letters to distinguish it from our trademark SPAM, which should be used with all uppercase letters.

As if uppercasing SPAM makes it something you'd welcome any more than e-mails from body-part-enhancing vendors. (For more information about how corporations want you to help them enforce their trademarks, see inta.org.)

AMERICAN ENGLISH IS ESCAPING ITS DICTIONARIES

It's a commonplace to say "the English language is always evolving," but the term *evolution* implies change so gradual that it can be observed only in retrospect—and that's not what's happening. The way we use language is changing so fast, coming (new terms and new meanings for old terms) and going (old distinctions), that even the most conscientious editors and writers have trouble knowing when, whether, or how to standardize the variations.

First-ever, one-of-a-kind terms have been coined so fast and spread so ubiquitously that they've become clichés—just put an *e* in front of any word, and it's understood to mean "something that takes place electronically, most likely through the Internet," along with *I*, *i*, and *cyber* close behind as prefixes referring vaguely to the Internet and the technology associated with it.

And of course, we have the now almost clichéd variations on *extreme* ("a radical, intense, barrier-breaking activity") used to hype everything from extreme sports to "the poetics of extreme engagement," whatever that is.

The result is new vocabulary that may not show up in any dictionary, which falls into six commonly encountered types:

- **Eccentric capitalization and punctuation** (lowercased initial capital letters, uppercased midcaps, a mixture of both, special characters) are techniques meant to imply that the latest and greatest and cutting-edgiest of technologies are at work. Thus, a program to publicize the achievements of people with handicaps called **disAbility**, and a reading and literacy initiative tries to inspire enthusiasm by calling itself **L!BRARY.** Terms are squooshed together in a rush, with or without internal capitalization: **GoToMeeting** (videoconferencingsoftware), **HarperCollinsBusiness** (book publisher), **WarCraft** (e-game). Do we respect the mark owner's style and include the punctuation no matter where it falls in the sentence? Or do we impose our style on the company's trademark?
- **Compounds** abound—should it be *cyber cash* or *cybercash*? *Website* or *Web site*? *Bunker buster* or *bunkerbuster* (bomb)? *Roller blades* or *rollerblades*? *Cell phone* or *cellphone*? *Land line* or *landline*?
- **Abbreviated forms** may be quirky but obvious and literal (*RLSI:* Ridiculously Large-Scale Integration), while others are illogical (*WNIC:* Wide-Area Network Interface Co-Processor) or just arbitrary *XML* (*eXtensible Markup Language*). Other abbreviations have become standard informal shorthand in and outside their niches: *social* for social security number, *SecDef* for Secretary of the Defense Department, *subprimes* for subprime mortgages or lenders.
- **Back-formations** and coinages take root, troubling mainly traditional editors, who bristle at parts of speech swapping out their traditional functions. New terms invented on the fly—like *exoneree*, someone found to be falsely imprisoned and freed of charges—and nouns used as verbs and vice versa, *–ize* forms, and otherwise morphed uses can be efficient, lively shorthand. Or not: *grow* a business, *transition* to a new job, *productivize* a capability, *gift* someone.
- **Retronyms** are created to handle new technologies and products, and new uses of old ones—so that even wireless landlines may ring but cellphones have tones, and inline skates and roller blades must be differentiated from ice and regular roller skates.

Some usage is meant purely to shock, show off, seem cutting-edge. We can't print off-color examples here; this is a family style guide. But here's a tame example: *By e-enabling our product functionalities we will grow revenue and leverage our brand equity.* Wow, e-enabling product functionalities! A lot of that sort of jargon can backfire; it comes to sound as quaintly "futuristic" as "Beam me up, Scotty!"

But innovative usage is also meant to help us take in new ideas and rethink familiar things. We should not be afraid or reflexively disdainful of such writing as this, by Barbara Kingsolver, in an except from her article for *Orion* magazine (orionmagazine.org), "Stalking the Vegetannual." She is advocating that people eat fruits and vegetables in season rather than importing them (using much fossil fuel) from around the globe:

> In many social circles it's ordinary for hosts to accommodate vegetarian guests, even if they're carnivores themselves. Maybe the world would like-wise become more hospitable to diners who are queasy about fuel-guzzling foods, if that preference had a name. Petrolophobes? Seasonaltarians? Lately I've begun seeing the term "locavores," and I like it: both scientifically and socially descriptive, with just the right hint of *livin' la vida loca.*
>
> Slow Food International has done a good job of putting a smile on this eating style, rather than a pious frown, even while sticking to the quixotic agenda of fighting overcentralized agribusiness.

We're all in favor of that kind of inventive writing. It's the stuff that leaves us in the dust and makes the uninitiated feel not only uninitiated but unwelcome that we've got to watch out for.

ARE WE BABBLING OUR WAY TO INCOHERENCE?

The pace of creating language matched to technological advances sometimes precludes reasoned consideration of how to treat a new form—by the time you've figured out whether to capitalize it, how to hyphenate it, or whether to even allow it, you may be describing a technology on its way out.

Does a general tolerance for—if not laissez-faire indifference toward—new usage really reflect a higher speed limit for daily life? Are we engaged in failing to communicate, at unprecedented speed? Are consistent spelling, style, and usage inevitable casualties of the drive toward a multitasking, tech-nosavvy culture with little time for editorial niceties? Does quality control for standard American English matter the way we used to think it did—or matter at all?

Even though we may not be able to cite chapter and verse from a text-book, we native speakers apply "the rules" of grammar and word formation to new terms almost without thinking. And we can look for such patterns of sim-ilarity as models for styling unfamiliar terms for our readers.

It's when we stop to think about neologisms that we start getting con-fused, like the fabled caterpillar who could walk just fine until someone asked him how he kept track of all those legs. Yet we *have* to stop and think about terms for which we may have no personal precedent—like *incentivize*, *bioneering*, and *anti-aliasing*.

How is a coinage functioning as a part or different parts of speech? If we allow the verb *incentivize* ("rewarding workers monetarily for performance," which is not the same as *monetize*, which means "to cause to earn revenue"), must we allow the cut form *incent*? (You will see it, but EEI Press editors implore you to disallow it.)

What are some nearly analogous terms we can use as precedents? We know the term *engineering*; can we assume readers will understand what the similar term *bioneering* means? But no—orthographic likeness can be a red herring. The meaning likely to be inferred—"biological engineering"—isn't correct. And good luck finding a succinct definition, even on the Web. A Google search finally brought us to this gloss by Jon Spayde, in a roundup of groundbreaking ideas listed in *Utne Reader*:

> A bioneer is a biological pioneer, an ecological inventor who's got an elegant and often simple set of solutions for environmental conundrums. The term comes from the pen of Kenny Ausubel, co-founder of Seeds of Change, a company that conserves and sells seeds for native plants that have been overshadowed by mega-agriculture's mighty, and unsustainable, hybrids.... Under the umbrella of their nonprofit Collective Heritage Institute, he and partner Nina Simons run the annual Bioneers Conference, where, since 1990, crowds of green problem-solvers have gathered to share their knowledge.
>
> Who are the bioneers? John Todd creates "living machines" that use various plants to carry out simple miracles of waste treatment. Vinnie McKinney's Elixir Farms gathers and preserves neglected and rare strains of medicinal herbs, particularly herbs used in Chinese medicine. John Roulac researches worthwhile uses for that infamous "weed," hemp. The list goes on, but what unites bioneers is the belief that in paying attention to how nature works, we can find the best ways to heal nature.

Even when definitions can be found more easily in technical glossaries, will readers know what *anti-aliasing* means from context, or should we define it at first use as "a process that removes jagged edges from onscreen type and images containing lines or curves"? Or will that seem condescending to knowledgeable readers—and annoy them? How can we know what level of language to use with readers when it's up to each of us individually to become aware of new terms?

Meaning aside, will readers need a hyphen to know how to pronounce an unfamiliar compound—or a term formed with a prefix that places the same two vowels adjacent, like *anti-aliasing*—or should we follow instances we find of *antialiasing*? Will we be thought old-fashioned for not using the solid form? Or puzzle readers to whom it looks like some sort of typo?

We have to make judgment calls about what's in the best interest of our readers. That's hard to do if we ourselves—editors and writers and quality control gatekeepers—don't keep an eye out for new terms. There's no magical way to do that: You've got to go on the Web, look at a variety of documents, and Google terms you're unfamiliar with. So be careful before editing a term you're unfamiliar with; what may seem like plain English to you may feel dumbed-down and naïve to the people who practice the art, craft, and Zen (not necessarily in that order) of bioneering, anti-aliasing, and incentivizing.

No special postmodern attitude is required to balance speedy innovation (a cultural inevitability) with consistency that shows concern for reader comprehension (professionally admirable—and a good business move). The trick, of course, is knowing which is which is which is which—and when to make up your own damned rules.

We show a healthy respect for the time and intelligence of readers when we make thoughtful decisions about style and usage—walking a fine line between rigidity and laissez-faire. As *Read Me First! A Style Guide for the Computer Industry* reminds us, "Consistency is not just some abstract goal to be achieved for its own sake; rather, the intention is to reduce the impact of the mechanics of communication on readers." But the basics still matter, and most traditional usage distinctions are still worth conserving.

Even though there will not always be a perfectly consistent resolution for every usage quirk in all major linguistic problem categories, please remember that it *is* the thoughtful attempt that counts, and do not become discouraged. If you do become discouraged, send your questions to us at press@eeicom.com and we'll try to help. We mean it: When in doubt, do not suffer in silence. Ask for help. Martyrdom is *so* old-fashioned.

ABBREVIATIONS, ACRONYMS, AND INITIALISMS

Abbreviations (the generic term) are meant to be a time- and space-saving form of shorthand, but they travel with a fair amount of stylistic baggage and cause editors and readers to do a lot of mental heavy lifting. And though we know that cryptic sets of letters can puzzle and annoy readers, for government, sci-tech-med, and military communicators especially, it's not an option to avoid them. Combating an enemy takes knowing its ins and outs, so let's look at good practices when you must engage it:

Two main types of abbreviations are used to represent a longer name or phrase:

- Acronyms are formed from the first letter or letters of a group of words. Acronyms can be pronounced as a word (e.g., *ASCII* is said as AS-key).
- Initialisms are also formed from the first letter or letters of a group of words. But initialisms are pronounced letter by letter (e.g., *IBM* is said as I-B-M).

Of course, the pronunciation of abbreviations isn't always so cut-and-dried (and how do you know if you've never heard a term pronounced?), and there are hybrids like *TIAA-CREF*—with the initial letters "T-I-A-A" pronounced separately and CREF treated as a word. *CD-ROM* is another such term. The more common if inexact term seems to be *acronym*, so we'll use it in the following discussions to mean all abbreviations, including initialisms.

To Define or Not to Define?

That's one of the first questions that arise with regard to acronyms. Here, as in so many areas, you must apply some judgment. One person's alphabet soup is another person's everyday speech. Would you rather be considered condescending or arrogant? Sometimes it seems that those are the choices. In an article for an employee newsletter, it would probably be silly to spell out the name of every department, if everyone in the company routinely refers to human resources as *HR*, research and development as *R&D*, or the like. A national press release from the same company should err on the side of caution by assuming that some readers will be stumped by such acronyms.

The high-tech world is rapidly catching up with the military as the number-one coiner of acronyms. Some, such as *modem*, have already undergone what's called *acronymy*—the process by which abbreviations come to be perceived and used as words. If you referred to a component that converts digital signals to sounds and back again as a *modulator/demodulator*, few people would know what you were talking about. (*Modem,* by the way, is an example of a syllabic acronym—formed from the first syllables of the basic term, rather than initial letters. More recent examples include *pixel,* short for picture element, and *codec,* short for coder-decoder.)

WYSIWYG, on the other hand, is listed in *Merriam-Webster's Collegiate Dictionary,* 11th edition, but still written in all capitals—a sign that its assimilation is not yet complete. Today, a computer magazine needn't bother to define it; some general-interest publications perhaps still should. In a couple of years, though, defining it may be as unnecessary as defining *IRS, FBI,* or *COB.*

So what do you do now? Even the editors of the *Chicago Manual of Style* have been known to say, in answer to questions posted on the manual's FAQ Web page, "We're waiting till the dust settles on this one." Try saying that you're waiting for consensus to magically emerge next time you're editing or writing a manuscript for publication, on deadline.

Here's what to do when you don't know what to do and the authorities fail you: You've got to make a decision, based on what you know about the context and about your readers.

"Know your readers" is the catchphrase in deciding which acronyms to define on first use. Here's another guideline: When in doubt, spell it out. Even if 90 percent of your readers know what URL stands for, the other 10 percent will be grateful to find out without having to stop and look it up. Of course, the newer an acronym is, the more important it is to define it, unless your audience is a crowd known to be Web-conversant and would see overdefinition as editorial amateurism. (This is one of many times you'll have to make an educated guess about such matters.)

Is there a difference in how you use acronyms when you're writing for the Web? The answer is yes. The Web writing chapter describes some of the physical differences involved in reading material in print and onscreen. These differences imply that you should use acronyms sparingly. Your readers may not have time to familiarize themselves with acronyms as they quickly browse, may not encounter the place where they are defined, and may not follow the jump to a definition link. An even more basic reason: Clusters of capital letters detract from readability, in print and online.

When you encounter a new acronym, how do you find out what it means? General-purpose acronym dictionaries run to multiple volumes, are outdated before they're printed, and are not very useful for defining short acronyms, since anything less than four letters is apt to have a couple hundred possible definitions. It's better to use a subject-specific reference. See the Resources for Continuing Education appendix for selected online references you may find useful.

Using Articles with Acronyms

In general, you can simplify your life by leaving off articles (*a, an, the*) with acronyms. For example, *IEEE publishes about a fourth of the world's electrical and computer engineering papers* (where *IEEE* is the Institute of Electronics and Electrical Engineers). If you do use them, you must be aware not only of the acronym's meaning, but of whether it's an acronym or an initialism—whether people familiar with the term pronounce it as a word or a string of letters. For example, the acronym SME (subject matter expert) is common in technical writing. Do you use *an* (as in *an S-M-E*) or *a* (as in *a smee*)? Turns out it's pronounced *smee*. URL also takes *a*—it's pronounced U-R-L. The conundrum arises with any acronym that starts with F, H, I, L, M, N, R, S, U, or X.

Capitalizing Definitions

In general, acronyms are written in all caps, without periods. Note, however, that when you define an acronym, the words themselves are not capitalized unless they represent a proper name. Compare *WYSIWYG* (what you see is what you get) with *ASCII* (American Standard Code for Information Interchange). Sometimes it can be tricky to ascertain whether the term is considered proper; you may see *HTML* (Hypertext Markup Language) spelled out with or without initial caps. It's a protocol name, and it should be uppercased.

Obviously, the consensus tack doesn't work for arbitrary, proprietary terms. You just need to have a good computer dictionary handy—or some bookmarks to specialized glossaries online. Having a friend in the IT department doesn't hurt. And you'd definitely benefit from creating a personal style sheet (or online style guide) to help you manage the specialized terms you're most likely to encounter.

As noted, an acronym may eventually be accepted as a word, in which case it sheds its capitals. But some acronyms that aspire to the status of words may find their place already taken—IT (information technology) is unlikely to be written *it*, no matter how familiar the term becomes.

Overlapping Acronyms

It's sloppy practice and potentially confusing to use a single acronym to represent more than one term. If you define IS as "information services," don't use it to mean "information systems" as well. Spell out the term that's less used or less commonly represented by an acronym.

Singular and Plural Acronyms

Most acronyms are singular in meaning. You form the plural just as you would for a word—by adding a lowercase *s*. One *CD-ROM*, two *CD-ROMs*. But a few are plural by definition, such as *WMD* (weapons of mass destruction). Some editors say there's no need to add an "s" to such acronyms—but will readers "think" plural or will it look as though you've made a typo when they see a plural verb with a singular-looking acronym? If you're making a plural form of an initialism that isn't written in all caps, use an apostrophe for the sake of clarity, as in *abc's* and *p's* and *q's*.

Abbreviations

Abbreviations range from the commonplace (Mr., Mrs.) to the esoteric (kbps). As these examples demonstrate, it's harder to generalize about the capitalization and punctuation of abbreviations than about acronyms and initialisms. You must be precise, especially when the abbreviation represents a unit of measure. For example, *kb* stands for kilobit, *kbps* for kilobits per second; *kB* stands for kilobyte, *kBps* for kilobytes per second. (All are measures of speed, just as *mph* is.)

Like other neologisms, abbreviations are proliferating. Many are informal curtailments of words that go from being used in conversation to being seen in print, such as *app* for application and *sig* for signature.

As for defining them, the same guidelines as for acronyms apply. Define any abbreviations that are likely to be unfamiliar to most of your readers. In a technical text laden with abbreviations and acronyms, it may make sense to provide a glossary in addition to or instead of in-text definitions. And remember, a glossary doesn't have to be the last item the reader sees. If it's essential to an understanding of the text, put it up front. In a document published on the Internet, you can link each abbreviation to its definition.

Capitalization

It's easy to say "capitalize proper nouns" and "treat brand names the way the owners treat them." But trying to follow these rules is far from simple. Is LISTSERV a proper noun? (The answer is yes.) If so, what is its generic equivalent—assuming it has one? (Electronic mailing list.) If a brand name begins with a lowercase letter, what happens when it's the first word in a sentence? Is there an authoritative source for the spelling and capitalization of brand names and trademarks?

WHAT'S PROPER?

It's the ***Internet***, also called ***the Net***. It's not the ***World Wide Web*** any longer but ***the Web***. These are proper nouns and should hang on to their capitals, as far as we're concerned—and that seems to be the mainstream consensus. So when you use *Web* as a modifier, retain the capital. A location on the Web is a *Web site* or *Web page*. But when you use *web* as a prefix, lowercase it. A person (male or female—sorry, we're not going to split feminist hairs over this one) who maintains a Web site is a *webmaster*. A magazine published exclusively on the Web is a *webzine* (also called an *e-zine*). On the other hand, your company, my company, and the company on the floor below us can each have its own *intranet*, so the term is not capitalized.

BUSINESS NAMES AND TRADEMARKS

Capitalization of business names, trademarks, and service marks should follow the owner's preference. But sometimes that's tricky to ascertain. In the good old days, you were fairly safe using headline-style capitalization (capitalizing the first letter of each "important" word). Now, lots of manufacturers are using midcaps (capitalizing seemingly random letters inside a name instead of only the first letter or significant letters) and eccentric punctuation to make product names stand out.

It's not safe to take your guidance solely from other publications, such as computer magazines that review new products. You have no way of knowing how carefully they've done their research. Perhaps the best resource for questions of spelling and capitalization of new products is on the Net itself—specifically, on the owner's site. Announcements of new products should appear there with the names accurately reproduced. In addition, you'll find "how to contact us" information, so you can follow up by e-mail or phone if necessary.

Many corporate sites publish a legal, copyright, or trademarks instruction page to help users accurately render the marks and names they own (service marks, product names, logos, etc.) and comply with restrictions on their use. In theory, you should be able to trust an owner's site to represent the spelling and capitalization of its own marks faithfully, but some actually *don't*. Design enhancements may disregard strict typographical rendering; for example, on their Web sites, Basecamp project management software is spelled BASE-CAMP, and on its site E*TRADE also wants to stand tall, with graphic mid-punctuation as well.

You can try e-mailing the public relations, marketing, or legal department for an authoritative answer when editorial and graphic treatments are inconsistent—if you have that kind of time. Many editors agree that, when a common keyboard character will accomplish a stylized spelling, it's easy enough to honor the preference. But editors who follow Associate Press style say that all special characters will be ignored or replaced to keep things simple for readers: **Library** (not L!brary or L!BRARY), **Basecamp**, **E-Trade** it is.

When referring to your own trademarked products, use the ® symbol for a registered trademark, the ™ symbol for an unregistered trademark, and the SM symbol for a service mark. Use them prominently whenever you mention the products; the use of the symbols reinforces your claims as rights holder.

But if you're not the mark holder, you're under no legal obligation to use those symbols. Just spell and capitalize the names of products and print them as nearly like the original marks as you reasonably can. Since owners have enlisted novel capitalization and punctuation to distinguish their products, however, you're going to be faced with some bizarre-looking constructions.

What if you want to begin a sentence with *eBay* or end it with *Yahoo!*? (Note the need for a question mark after the exclamation point.) The first choice is to try to avoid the issue by reworking the sentence. If that fails, retain the name's idiosyncrasies. And if you can't stand the way the resulting sentence looks, go back to square one—now you have even more incentive to figure out a way to reword it:

Instead of:	eBay is a popular online auction service.
Try:	One popular online auction service is eBay.

Instead of:	Do you use the search engine Yahoo!?
Try:	Is Yahoo! one of the search engines you use?

Yahoo! itself uses the tagline "Do you Yahoo!?" It's an infinitely concentric set of silliness we get ourselves into with such trademarked end-punctuation games. It's enough to bring on an attack of *e-ennui.*

PERSONAL TITLES

This is another area in which the old rules are being bent. The trend toward downstyle means lowercasing personal titles, even when they precede a person's name:

> chief information officer Wang Lee (abbreviation: CIO)
> content provider Rolf Stuart
> sysadmin Adrian Lowry (short for system administrator)

PREFIXES

High-tech communications are spawning prefixed terms as fast as they're spawning acronyms. The evolutionary trend in English is to go from hyphenating prefixes to writing them closed up, or solid. The question is, how quickly does the process occur? And how can you know when a term should be considered a permanently solid? Well, to some degree we're all making these terms up as we go—and each decision is a vote leading toward consensus.

The speed of communications media is contributing to linguistic change—some writers figure that since the hyphen will disappear eventually, they might as well dispense with it at the outset. Thus, you see *e*business, *e*mail, *e*trade, and even *e*economics—as one ad used to say, *e*enough! In the case of single-letter prefixes, we recommend retaining the hyphen rather than rushing the process. For one thing, a single-letter prefix tends to look strange without a hyphen—sort of like pig latin. It upsets spell checkers. And it may make readers stumble for a moment over pronunciation. Remember that hyphens are indeed meant as an aid to comprehension—not as decoration—and use them if in your best judgment your readers would look at a term like *digiilliteracy* and say "Huh?"

cyber- short for cybernetic. Generally closed up: *cybercafe, cybercash*™, *cyberpunk* (a subgenre of science fiction; the term was coined to describe William Gibson's seminal *Neuromancer,* published in 1984), *cybersex, cyberspace* (from *Neuromancer,* describing the "consensual hallucination" that is approximated by the World Wide Web), *cybersquatting* (registering domain names early in hopes of selling them to companies later on). However, if a coinage seems likely to be a one-time use, you may prefer not to close it up: "Welcome to Cyber Purgatory."

digi- short for digital. Like *e-* and *cyber-*, this prefix is used loosely, often to give a "hip" look to certain words. *Digibabble, digirati,* and *digitocracy* are soundalike coinages whose meanings are easy to infer.

e- short for electronic. Implies "done over the Internet." Keep the hyphen in generic terms: *e-banking, e-business, e-commerce, e-mail, e-text.* Also frequently used in product names: *eBay, ePaper.*

hyper- *hyperlink, hypertext.* Refers to the system that enables readers to jump from one document to another on the Internet. The dictionary definition of *hyper* is "excessive," and the use of links may verge on the excessive.

i- short for Internet. Same implication as *e-*. Slightly less common than *e-*, but used the same way. It may be used as the prefix for a Web site name (*iParenting, iVillage*).

meta- short for a more highly organized, comprehensive, or specialized version of a discipline of body of information: *meta-analysis, metadata, metatag.*

multi- short for multiple: *multitasking, multithreaded.*

techno- short for technical: *technobabble, technophile, technophobe.*

tele- short for distance. *Telephone* and *television* remind us of how quickly we assimilate new words formed with prefixes. Younger, but already almost as familiar, are such terms as *telecommute* and *teleconference.*

web- | Web- short for the World Wide Web. You have to be careful with this one, since sometimes it's a noun used as an adjective: *Web page, Web site, Web-related.* When *web* is used as a prefix, it isn't capitalized: *webcam, webmaster, webzine.*

SUFFIXES

Novel terms formed with suffixes aren't nearly so prevalent as those formed with prefixes. Perhaps, once we've tacked an e- on the front of every word in the language, we'll start relying more on suffixes.

-cast refers to a means of disseminating information: *broadcast, narrowcast, netcast, webcast.*

-tech from *technical: high-tech* (also seen as *hi-tech*), *low-tech.*

-ware from *software* and *hardware*, we go to *freeware, groupware, shareware,* and *wetware* (the brain). The plural *warez* (pronounced "wares") is used specifically to refer to computer software and hardware. Ware will we go next?

HYPHENS AND COMPOUNDING

Put any two words together and use them to describe a third, and you have a compound modifier. Put them together and use them to represent "a person, place, or thing," and you have a compound noun. The question is, how do you put them together? Do you join them with a hyphen? Do you keep them pristinely apart when they appear at the end of a sentence, but insert a hyphen when they precede the word they modify? Do you throw caution to the wind and weld them together immediately?

Trends and Patterns

The speed of electronic communications is accelerating certain trends in grammar. One of these trends is the tendency of terms to evolve from two words, to a hyphenated term, to one word. Some terms start and stay hyphenated. Some skip step one and maybe step two and go immediately to either a hyphenated form or a single word formed from two words.

Voicemail is good example. Some people are still writing it as two words; others have decided that it's one word. A few used a hyphen, but not many, and not for very long. Below are some nouns we've seen used in various ways—we'll go out on a limb and say we now prefer the solid form for *voicemail*:

click through	click-through	clickthrough
home page	home-page	homepage
news group		newsgroup
user group		usergroup
voice mail	voice-mail	voicemail

Another trend is to discard certain so-called rules that are difficult to apply. One of these is the rule for hyphenating unit modifiers depending on their position in a sentence. Traditionally, such modifiers are hyphenated only if they precede the word they modify—unless the hyphenated form is used so frequently that it is considered a permanent compound. Here's an example:

I like to invest in *high-tech stocks.*

Some of these *companies* are so *high tech* that I don't understand what they do.

Today, however, many writers are impatient with this rule; they believe that if a compound term is likely to become permanent, it should always be hyphenated. When speed is of the essence, they reason, who has time to fiddle with guessing where finicky hyphens are on the chart? See eeicom.com/press/compounds.html for a list of terms we consider to be permanent compounds, and an article on how to recognize the various categories of compounds.

MORPHING PARTS OF SPEECH

When writers coin a new word, one way to decide how to treat it is to see what existing word(s) it resembles. *E-tailing* was coined on the base word *retailing*, for example. Yet another characteristic of our language is our ability to form verbs from nouns and vice versa. And—guess what?—such mutations are happening faster than ever. Is *e-mail* a noun or a verb? In all but the most formal writing, it's both. *I'll e-mail my reply. I just received your e-mail.*

A *cookie* is an identifier that Web marketers can use to identify computers that visit their sites. Overheard in a conversation, the phrase "We'll cookie you" passed without the listener exhibiting visible tremors of discomfort. But the speaker probably would not have written it the same way—or would he?

So if you encounter a word being used as a part of speech that isn't assigned to it in the dictionary, it may not be wrong; it may simply be new. Comfort levels differ; when this sort of sporting spoken language is asked to sit still in print, it loses some of its verve. A little of it goes a long way in all but the most genuinely, strenuously geeky publications (for example, *shift* magazine).

The words below have essentially the same meanings in their noun and verb forms. Some are relatively new; some have been around for quite a while. The list does not include words such as *port* that have different meanings as nouns and verbs:

access	e-mail	index	spam
address	hit	mail	spec
cache	host	modem	undo
chat	fax	post	upload
chunk	firewall	program	visit
download	FTP	search	

NUMBERS

There's no difference between "Internet style" and print style when it comes to numbers, except for the fact that research shows numerals are easier to read onscreen. If you're writing on technical or scientific topics, you're more likely to use figures for numbers above nine and for all units of measure. In general, whatever style you normally follow for print publications will work. The subject of information technology itself can entail discussion of very large numbers, which is where certain prefixes come in:

kilo (often k)—1 thousand
mega—1 million
giga—1 billion
tera—1 trillion

TYPESETTING URLS

How do you set a uniform resource locator (URL or Web address) in type? In general, URLs are not case-sensitive, so take the easy way and type them in lowercase letters.

For brevity, we now recommend omitting *http://* and *www.* It's preferable to set URLs on one line of type, without breaking them, but that's often impossible. When you must break a URL, try to do so after a slash but before a period, to avoid the appearance of terminal punctuation. And don't insert a hyphen when breaking a URL; since internal punctuation is part of the address, adding a hyphen where it doesn't belong can misdirect readers.

When a sentence ends with a URL, it's pretty safe to use terminal punctuation. Even if readers misunderstand and assume that the period is part of the URL, almost all browsers will ignore the end punctuation and take them to the right place.

How about setting off URLs typographically? It's a question of style, not rock-ribbed right or wrong. Some publications set them in italics or bold italics. This has the advantage of making it easy to see where the URL begins and ends, although in practice that's usually pretty obvious. We recommend following older conventions: If you don't use a special type for a postal address or telephone number, why do it for a URL?

Microsoft Word automatically underlines anything it recognizes as a URL or an e-mail address, showing that the program has created a link to that address. In a Word file, you can double-click on such links and go from Word to the address in question. This fact has led many people to typeset URLs with an underscore. But that's an option, not a necessity.

STYLE FOR WORLDWIDE WRITING

The Web takes away geographical boundaries; unless you're writing for a subscription or members-only site, your work is available for viewing around the globe. Can you afford to be blind to this fact? Increasingly, the answer is no. The notion of having readers in Iceland, Serbia, Indonesia, and Ghana can be daunting—and should be inspiring, too.

Technical writers, in particular, are compelled to be aware of such issues as use of idioms that cannot be translated literally, cultural references that make no sense out of context, and even the use of certain colors in illustrations. Some companies have developed rigid vocabularies, with as many don'ts as dos (please note that it's not *do's*), to facilitate computer-assisted translation of technical documents. People who complain that such vocabularies are limiting miss the point. The vocabularies are not intended as tools of literature; they are designed to facilitate basic communication that will enable customers to use a product.

Even if you aren't constrained by the knowledge that your work will be translated into 25 languages, you can apply some commonsense global sensitivity to your writing for the Web. Here are a few points to bear in mind.

Abbreviations

If your Web content contains numerous abbreviations, acronyms, or initialisms, you may want to take a second look. Because readers see only a screenful of information at a time and may or may not read your entire document, the print technique of defining such terms on first mention won't always work. Consider spelling out terms you might ordinarily abbreviate, if you think readers won't know them. If it's essential to use abbreviations, create links to their explanations.

Currency

If you're referring to US dollars, say so. ("The book costs US $30.75.") Here's a list of countries that call their currency the dollar: Australia, the Bahamas, Barbados, Belize, Brunei, Canada, the Cayman Islands, Dominica, Fiji, Grenada, Guyana, Hong Kong, Jamaica, Kiribati, Liberia, Namibia, Nauru, New Zealand, St. Kitts-Nevis, St. Lucia, St. Vincent and the Grenadines, Singapore, the Solomon Islands, Taiwan, Trinidad and Tobago, Tuvalu, the United States, and Zimbabwe. There's plenty of overlap in other currencies, too (e.g., dinar, franc, peso). Use words rather than symbols, as well as the name of the country, if there is any likelihood of confusion. Using words also eliminates having to search for special symbols on your computer. If you're writing about a particular time, you might also want to add the year (1998 US dollars). Because currencies fluctuate constantly, it's not advisable to give equivalents in other currencies unless you're writing about the past.

Clock Times

Particularly if you know you're communicating with an international (or even a nationwide) audience, it's a good idea to specify a time zone if accuracy is crucial. Here again, spell it out. "The meeting will begin at 2:30 p.m., Eastern Standard Time." Technical or military readers, as well as many international audiences, are comfortable with the 24-hour clock: "The meeting will begin at 14:30, Eastern Standard Time." If you decide to go with this system, mention it, to avoid confusing some readers.

Dates

Abbreviations can lead to confusion. To you *2/6/01* may be February 6, but in European countries the date normally precedes the month, so readers may perceive it as June 2. For maximum clarity, write "February 6, 2001." If your writing is so full of dates that you think abbreviations are essential, give readers a brief explanation: "In this document, the day appears first, then the month, then the year. For example, 2/6/01 is June 2, 2001."

Of course, the above discussion isn't global either—it assumes a Christian (and, specifically, western, as opposed to Eastern Orthodox) calendar. January 1, 2000, didn't signal a new millennium (or the close of an old one, to be painfully precise) in India, where the year was 1921; in Israel, where it was 5749; or in Muslim countries, where it was 1420. However, unless you expect a sizable portion of your readership to be in one of those areas, it's safe to use the western calendar; most readers will understand it.

Numbers

There are two issues to consider: punctuation and numbers above one million. Where as the United States uses commas to punctuate figures larger than four or five digits, Germany and France, for example, use periods, and Sweden uses spaces. The period/comma dichotomy is more likely to lead to misunderstandings, since a period could be mistaken for a decimal point. If your writing contains just a few large numbers, spell them out to avoid confusion. Otherwise, give an explanation: "In this document, 1,000 equals one thousand; 1.00 equals one."

For numbers above one million, the arithmetic values actually diverge. For example, 1,000,000,000,000 is a trillion in the United States but a billion in Great Britain. *Merriam-Webster's Collegiate Dictionary*, 11th edition, gives a cogent explanation in its table of numbers. For scientific or technical writing, it's a good idea to use figures for such large numbers. If you spell them out, specify "US system," for example, after the words. Remember that numerals are easier to read onscreen than words for quantities.

Punctuation

American English punctuation differs from British punctuation. There's some disagreement as to whether you should adopt the latter for Web publications, assuming you don't use it for your print materials. If you can reasonably expect or are actively seeking an international audience, and particularly if your subject matter is technical, it's worth considering.

American: Double quotation marks for a primary quotation; single quotation marks for a quotation within a quotation. Terminal punctuation marks within quotation marks:

> After shouting, "This so-called 'disaster' is all just a misunderstanding," Roberts turned on his heel and stormed out, muttering, "I give up."

British: Single quotation marks for a primary quotation; double quotation marks for a quotation within a quotation. Terminal punctuation marks inside or outside quotation marks, depending on sense:

> After exclaiming, 'This so-called "disaster" is all just a misunderstanding!', Roberts turned on his heel and stormed out.

Units of Measure

Until the United States gets in step with the world, writing that includes the "English" system of measurement (which the English no longer use) will need to be translated into the metric system (also called the Système International, or SI). What's tricky is that one or the other set of measurements will be "off." There is no exact equivalency between units in the two systems, such as inches and centimeters, feet and meters. If it's crucial that your readers get the amounts right, you will need to measure in both systems rather than using a conversion formula. If a formula will do, there's some inexpensive shareware that you can install on your computer to take care of the math. Don't think it matters? Quick: If you're driving 60 kph, are you speeding or creeping? If it's 20°C, are you hot or cold?

"We"

We, the people of the United States, have a tendency to speak and write as if we were everyone. The words "America" and "Americans" grate on readers in Canada, Mexico, Central America, and South America when they're applied only to the United States and its citizens. And changing the phrase "this country" to "the United States" will make your writing clearer.

ELECTRONIC CITATIONS

More and more information is available in electronic format. Many sources are offered in both print and electronic form; some exist only as CD-ROMs or Web pages. The principle for citing electronic references is the same as that for citing print: Provide complete information that will enable the reader to locate the source.

The amount of information you need to give in text references will depend on whether you provide a formal bibliography. If you do, your in-text citation should resemble that for a print reference: Give the author (or title, if no author is available) and year of publication. For example, (Bunn, 2000) or ("A Beginner's Guide to HTML," 1996). Follow these guidelines for bibliographic entries:

- **Web sites.** Attribute material to the author or authors (if you can identify them) and then give the title, URL, and the date you accessed the Web site. The latter information is important because Web sites change frequently.

  Bunn, Austin. "Prisoner of Love." http://salon.com/ent/feature/2000/01/27/letourneau/index.html. (Jan. 27, 2000). [In this example, the URL includes the date the article was published online.]

  "The Living Pond." www.sover.net/~bland/pond.htm. (Jan. 27, 2000). [This example has no author listed.]

  Bray, Hiawatha. "DoubleClick's Double Cross." www.digitalmass.com/news/daily/0127/upgrade.html. (Jan. 27, 2000). [The URL includes the month and date, but not the year, of publication.]

- **E-mail.** Cite e-mail messages as personal correspondence. Do not include the e-mail address of your correspondent. Give the person's name (rather than the e-mail alias) if you know it. Where you would list the title of a publication, list the subject line of the e-mail message. Give the date the message was sent.

  Smith, John. "Woodchuck population in Rhode Island." June 30, 2000. Personal e-mail.

  Jsmith. "Woodchuck population in Rhode Island." June 30, 2000. Personal e-mail. [In this case, you know the correspondent's alias but not the real name.]

- **Electronic lists and newsgroups.** Because these lists are available to the public, messages received through them are not considered personal correspondence. They are, however, subject to copyright protection. In addition to the information you would cite for an e-mail message, include the name of the list or newsgroup, and both the date the message was posted and the date you accessed it.
- Baughman, David. "Re: [Q] A-Fib and cardioversion?" Jan. 21, 2000. AT&T WorldNet Services, sci.med.cardiology. (Jan. 27, 2000).
- **CD-ROM.** List the author's name if it is available, the title of the section or article, the title of the CD-ROM, and any other publication information that is available. Since CD-ROMs are less mutable than Web sites, do not list the date you accessed the material.

"A Beginner's Guide to HTML." *Microsoft Works & Bookshelf 1996–97.* Microsoft Corp., 1996. [This example has no author listed.]

You can deal with electronic references in electronic publications by providing a link to any references you cite. Such links eliminate the need to provide URLs, since readers can access the reference directly. *"Jack Powers* suggests that your Web site must attract search engines in order to attract readers" is the Web substitute for "Jack Powers, at electric-pages.com/articles/wftw2.htm (Feb. 2, 2000), suggests...." Bear in mind, however, that Web documents are transient. The link may not indefinitely take readers to the article you have in mind. Providing the URL is a more durable form of citation—though not eternal.

COPYRIGHT: CONTENT MIGHT YEARN TO BE FREE, BUT AUTHORS AND PUBLISHERS NEED TO MAKE A LIVING

Material published on the Internet is intellectual property and, as such, is protected by copyright. The fact that it's easy to copy the information does not alter the principles of ownership, any more than does the fact that photocopiers make it easy to copy printed materials. Even material posted on electronic mail groups is subject to copyright protection, although, since it may have no commercial value, the author of the material would have difficulty recovering financial damages for copyright violation.

When you publish a document on the Internet, it's a good idea to include a copyright notice, just as you would for a print publication. Doing so will make it easier to recover damages for copyright infringement. However, material that appears without such a notice is not in the public domain unless the owner specifically states that it is.

Remember, from a copyright point of view, publishing on the Internet is no different from publishing in print. The same rules of fair use apply. See the appendix of resources for continuing education for articles on fair use, online plagiarism, digital copyright legislation, and other related resources.

9

You've Got a Style of Your Own

Whether you're the style guardian of your own work or the resident style keeper (stylekeeper?) in a big shop, your aim is to make consistent calls using rationales that cover most cases. Guidelines that you formalize for yourself are *proprietary*—that is, they belong and apply solely to you. They can take the form of a simple alphabetical style sheet or a comprehensive guide, and they can be in a notebook, on an intranet, or on an extranet so contributing authors can access them. This section offers considerations for both print and electronic guides. Creating a style guide will definitely take time and effort, but once it exists, you'll wonder how you got along without it.

What are the advantages of creating a proprietary style guide or style sheet?

- **You create it, so it can be highly specific to your needs.** It's not about your company adapting to somebody else's style but about adapting a main style to fit your company. It's going to reflect your preferences, trademarks, and other special matters dictated by the legal liabilities or branding goals inherent in your publishing efforts. You don't have to care what styles other companies follow once you've made your own thoughtful (or eccentric—hey, it's your jargon!) decisions. Just be clear about what the sources for your standards are. Tell people something like this in a "how to use this guide section": "For matters not covered here, please refer to [*name and edition of published style guide*] or [*name and edition of dictionary*]. Everything listed in this guide reflects the consensus of senior management and the publications staff on what will best serve our audiences."
- **It can reflect a consensus that ensures it will be used.** You create it for your colleagues, so they should be asked to help make sure it contains the answers they need. Every organization has its own set of recurring questions—are *more than* and *over* synonyms now? (Yes, for most of us.)

Can we start a sentence with *And, Because, Or,* and *But?* (Yes, for more of us.) Do we refer to the school on a second reference as the *University* or the *university?* Ask everyone associated with writing, editing, and reviewing publications in your organization to give you a short list of terms or rules they feel uncertain about and iffy, inconsistent examples they've noticed in your publications. From the start, it can be pitched as a collaboration of everybody who cares about quality control. That's a good way to get people invested in successfully launching an organization-wide style guide.

- **It can reinforce your professional image—and that of your organization.**
It should reflect careful consideration of editorial and design attributes widely acknowledged to affect credibility and accessibility. Eliminating inconsistencies makes it less likely that readers will be distracted from the main message of the document. Even though many readers may not consciously recognize style inconsistencies and usage errors, they convey the impression that a document lacks polish—and possibly has cut substantive corners. By offering clients and consumers of your publishing products consistent quality, you and your organization are linked with impressions of credibility and know-how.

Creating a style sheet to cover the frequently encountered issues that require special handling in your publications may be enough to get you started on the road to a full-blown inhouse guide. In fact, the more succinct and specific your style guide, the more likely people are to use it. And fortunately, though creating or updating a style guide can be a major undertaking, you don't have to invent the process.

You can learn a lot from observing how major style guides are compiled— the magic words are *systematically* and *incrementally.* When it comes to the classic components of a style guide, you'll find they fall into these categories:

- **Word usage.** List dos and don'ts (e.g., "Refer to our organization as *the firm,* not *the company.*" "Refer to people who work for the firm as *associates,* not *employees.*"). Also list specific terms, such as the names of departments or publications. Standardize frequently confused terms: "Use *ensure* to mean *make certain* and *insure* to mean *cover with insurance.*"
- **Acronyms and abbreviations.** List and define those commonly used by your organization. Specify which ones *don't* need to be defined (such as *IRS* or *FBI*). Explain your stance on whether acronyms need to be preceded by an article, and show how to make acronyms plural (*PUDs* or *PUD's*).
- **Hyphenation.** List the treatment of frequently used terms that raise questions: Are they hyphenated, not hyphenated, or have they grown together

to form one word? Is it *day trading, day-trading,* or *daytrading? fiberoptic* or *fiber-optic? health care* or *healthcare? longer-term agreement* or *longer term agreement?*

- **Capitalization.** A style guide needn't instruct writers to capitalize the first word in a sentence or people's names, but it should point out certain pitfalls. For example, "Capitalize job titles before, but not after, a person's name: *Chief Executive Officer Smith,* but *Mary Smith, chief executive officer.*" "Do not capitalize the words *table* and *figure* in text: *See figure 2.*" "Capitalize the first word following a colon if the phrase is a complete sentence; otherwise, lowercase it." List specific terms that should always be capitalized, and terms with unique capitalization: *1stUp.com.*

- **Punctuation.** The main discretionary items are the use of serial commas *(Tom, Dick and Harry* versus *Tom, Dick, and Harry)* and punctuation of lists. Many writers use dashes (em dash, en dash, and hyphen) inconsistently, so examples of correct use can be helpful. The punctuation section, like the grammar section, may grow as people submit questions about what they find confusing. Ask for example sentences that show the problem in context.

- **Numbers.** There's a lot of latitude in using figures versus words. You can simply reference your default published style (e.g., "Use *Chicago* style for numbers"), but it helps to provide examples drawn specifically from your organization's topics. This section can cover the use of numbers in text and in lists, tables, and sidebars, as well as basic rules: "Round up to whole numbers in comparisons" and "Don't start a sentence with a figure."

- **References.** If you publish references, your house style should give a few typical examples (e.g., book, journal, Web site) along with a reference to your default style. Cover in-text callouts, bibliographic listings, and possibly footnote style. Remind writers that global search/replace functions should *not* be applied to references. Your house style may be to use serial commas and US spellings. But applying those guidelines could distort the title of a work published in the United Kingdom, for example. Preserve the original spelling and punctuation of titles listed in references.

- **Grammar.** By definition, a style guide isn't a grammar text. Nonetheless, a few cogent examples can save people a lot of trouble. One way to home in on the problems that trip people up is to ask your editorial staff what grammatical errors they often correct in the work they review. If you post a brief grammar section on your intranet, it will grow as people submit questions—especially if you do informal surveys. And you can encourage your writers to consult this section and ask questions. Perhaps the most vexing question in grammar is that of subject/verb agreement for collective nouns: *A small percentage/a number of people/the majority* **is** or **are?** Provide a rule and several examples to illustrate it.

- **Format.** Not all style guides address format. In the interest of brevity, you may prefer to present format guidelines in a separate document. But if your writers are producing documents that go straight from their computers to your readers, you may need to treat format as intrinsic to style.

How many types of documents do your writers produce? You may want to provide electronic templates for the most common ones. For a large organization with many departments, each of which has been producing documents with its own format, the creation of a house style can be the opportunity to achieve consistency. But beware: Format can be a contentious issue if you don't have corporate style or branding guidelines to follow. Format includes both editorial and design considerations. Here are some of them:

- Type choices—font defaults and permissible combinations
- Levels of headings
- Running headers and footers
- Logos
- List style
- Table and figure style and file format
- Address information (telephone numbers, state abbreviations)

Case Study: Using a Macro to Check for Biased Language

Problem: A large national organization needed a way for staff members to check for and correct unintentionally biased language in a wide variety of business communications. Although memos informed staff of the need to check for potentially biased terms, it was difficult for everyone to remember and correct the hundreds of terms that could be problems. The company decided to have a programmer create a macro that would search for and replace problem words. But although some problem words could be corrected through a simple search and replace—for example, changing *deaf and dumb* to *deaf* or *hearing impaired*—others required more intervention. For example, changing *handicapped* to *person with a disability* in the sentence *This is an excellent guide for handicapped people* required the writer to manually delete *people*.

Solution: The programmer created a macro that functioned like a spelling checker. The writer clicked a button to activate the macro, and the macro searched the document for problem words from a predetermined list. When the macro located a problem word, the writer could read the text, choose from suggested replacement words shown by the macro, and make the appropriate substitution. If necessary, the writer could pause the macro and edit the text, then restart the macro to continue checking the document. The macro was distributed on diskettes and was easy to install.

- Fax and report cover sheets
- E-mail signatures
- Colors for branding pieces (letterhead, report binding, leave-behind fact sheets and brochures, press kit folders), presentations, and Web sites

Case Study: Using a Macro to Convert Tables

Problem: A publishing company produced more than 60 newsletters a week and needed a way to quickly strip the electronic files of extraneous layout codes and convert them to multiple coded text files (including HTML) that could be sent electronically to news wires. Because of the fast turnaround, the accuracy required by the news wires, and the high error rate of the manual process, the company needed a faster, more economical, more reliable way to process the files. A programmer created a macro that would turn these newsletters into working coded text files. One challenge was converting tables. The company had many different table formats but, on its own, the macro could recognize only one type of table. For example, one table might have headings down each row that should instead be at the top of each column, while another table might be the opposite, and still another might be one large table broken into smaller tables. How can the macro tell the difference?

Solution: It can't—but the editor can. The programmer devised a macro to act as an interactive menu. The editor can highlight a table and click a key to activate the macro. A menu prompts the editor with a list of possible table types. The editor clicks a button for the desired type, and the macro converts the table appropriately. If this isn't what the editor wanted after all, the original table is retrieved, and the editor is again presented with the menu of options. This macro was part of a larger text conversion macro and was distributed through the company's network on the editors' computers.

MAKING SPECIFIC EDITORIAL CHOICES

Within reason, you can designate as "officially correct" the editorial choices that seem right to your eye and ear. Wherever alternatives exist, you'll need to provide users of your guide with examples that offer guidance in context—that means in the context of the sorts of documents they will be writing and editing.

One way to be sure your guide is relevant to your style issues is to test it before distributing it to everyone or going live. Have a few editors work through it critically, and ask a few editors, writers, and managers to try using it for a month or so. Ask them to note what helped and what didn't. As they encounter omissions, mistakes, and incomplete cross-references to related material, your beta-testers will give you a chance to strengthen the usefulness and accuracy of the guide. And you're setting a precedent for updating the guide; you'll need all the feedback you can get from now on, so you might as well make it part of the culture.

Successful corporate style guides have these characteristics in common:

- They are short and to the point. They stick to the areas not covered by published style manuals, or those where the organization's style diverges from published style manuals (e.g., capitalizing "Firm" when referring to the organization).
- They get buy-in from users before they are released.
- They are introduced to the organization with enough fanfare that people realize they are to be taken seriously.
- They are updated frequently enough that users regard the advice as current and reliable.
- They are presented and viewed as helpful tools, not as weapons to use against those who don't conform.

Here's a suggested list of priorities once you've got agreement that a proprietary guide is called for and you're the lucky one designated to create it:

- Set up a committee of the people most qualified to identify the points of confusion, research the options, and make editorial decisions. "Most qualified" means wide (not necessarily long) experience as a hands-on writer or editor and a flexible outlook that will allow them to make pragmatic decisions instead of going ballistic because something "isn't in Webster's."
- Ask everyone who produces documents to meet for 30 minutes to kick off the planning stage. Ask for a few volunteers right then and there to help prepare and send out a companywide e-mail survey of "things that drive you nuts or worry you most," compile results, and set the stage for recommendations.
- Target the most frequently cited style problems for immediate remedy and circulate draft guidelines for review by everyone who prepares documents, not just management. (Remember to include the layout and production specialists.) Ask for comments.
- Collate comments and distribute "final" style decisions and some examples by e-mail or paper memo. Congratulations! You have begun preparing a guide by treating the most irritating editorial hotspots.
- Working with management and your art director or senior design staff, begin formalizing editorial and graphic standards that everyone who prepares documents should be aware of.
- Make templates of letterhead logos, addresses, taglines, trademarks, and document formats (memo, fax cover sheets, letter bids, formal proposals) available to all staff on the intranet.

- Ask whoever performs copyediting and quality control reviews to make note of or keep copies of the style problems they see most often. These are likely to be the areas people need most education about—because they don't know when to spell out numbers, they have the rules wrong ("There's no difference between *ensure* and *insure*"), or they don't know that there *is* a style decision to be made about capitalization of the first word of a clause after a colon.

- Compile these refinements and nitty-gritty examples and distribute them to everyone for comment. Ask people to look for examples of when the rules don't work or just tell you whether they "like" the rules you propose. You may not change the rules, but giving people a chance to be grouchy now can pay off later—down the road, you don't want to hear "Why should I do it that way? 'Our' style, huh? Nobody asked *me* about it."

- Start planning the best way to get a copy of the complete set of guidelines on every desk or computer, and set a schedule for regular reviews and updates. Keep asking people to give you examples of problems from their work that need resolution so style decisions can leave the world of anecdote and personal preference and become part of the guide.

- Thank everyone, personally and publicly, who has contributed to the guide.

- Don't let down your guard. A style guide is always a work in progress and will need revision as often as your organization repositions itself, adds jargon for new processes, and redesigns itself.

- Make sure to tell people whenever you depart from your designated main style guide and main dictionary—and make sure people have copies of your base references within easy reach for filling the gaps in your guidelines as you continue to build them. Better to have people making somewhat consistent decisions in the meantime about, say, when to hyphenate or close up new compounds, even if you are still in the process of making changes to be more consistent with other in-house style decisions.

- When new editions of your default style guide and dictionary are published, get new copies for your office. The Associated Press style guide, for example, is updated annually—not so much because its rules change, but because it needs to keep up with names and terms in the news.

PROPRIETARY STYLES AT WORK

To get a sense of the range of editorial and graphics details that a style may encompass, it's revealing to see editors at work making style decisions in context. Here are a few examples of editors:

- The managing editor of an IBM magazine for AS/400 computer users met every six months with her staff to discuss the acronyms most frequently used in the publication. They tried to decide which ones are so commonly used in the industry that they don't need to be spelled out, even at first reference. Some of the acronyms on their list were API, CPU, FTP, LAN, SQL, IT, and ISP. They worried that not all readers would know what those terms meant, but they're used over and over in every issue and can't be repeatedly redefined. This is an ongoing struggle for the magazine's staff: serving less-savvy readers while keeping copy uncluttered for advanced users.
- *The Editorial Eye* newsletter, like many periodicals, has a style sheet adapted from the simplest rules of several major styles, in a mix both conservative and forward-looking. State abbreviations are postal-style (all caps), and the adjective *US* follows international style in leaving off the periods, as for the UK. Many terms that *Merriam-Webster's Collegiate Dictionary*, 11th edition, and other guides show as two words (open or hyphenated) are rendered as solid compounds to reflect more contemporary usage (*badmouth, onsite, freelancer, copyedit, lifestyle, online, kneejerk*). And style is emphatically down even for titles preceding a proper name (*Wistar Institute president and CEO Russel E. Kaufman, MD*). The *Eye*'s editors have let go of the *since–because, if–whether,* and *more than–over* distinctions, but they hold the line against such "modern" gaffes as hyphenating *-ly* adverbs (*The barely-tasted cookie fell to the floor*) and such misusages as *a myriad of, comprised of,* and the nugatory *as such.*

That's really what we're trying to do with style guidance: help editors and writers and designers lose their uncertainty so readers and users won't be bothered by unnerving little discrepancies and holes.

MAKING INTRANET CONTENT EASY TO USE

Which is more frustrating to people in search of help with style: having to flip through pages of badly organized and cryptically indexed rules, or having to scroll through long screenfuls of unsearchable items with many irrelevant links to get to the point? It's a wash. Very few people read style guides for fun.

What you'll learn here about online navigation has implications for print, too. It's hard to beat great categorical organization and a great index, and it's hard to beat an intelligent keyword search capability based on HTML with supplemental material in a PDF to show examples of graphics (forms, list styles, address formats, acceptable color and fonts, logos, and the like). In both mediums, these are the most important things to build in:

- Recognizable lists or categories of problems and choices
- Logically cross-referenced answers that can be located quickly
- Examples that make distinctions, exceptions, and applications clear

One of the biggest challenges in writing an online style guide is placing intelligent links. The trick is to embed them in the natural conversational flow of a statement—the *Yale Style Guide* calls it *parenthetical placement*—so the link makes logical sense without interrupting.

Avoid saying, "Click here for more examples of dangling modifiers." Avoid giving the imperative "Click," period. Why? It's distracting—when someone is trying to find information, it's annoying to be commanded to go somewhere else for it.

Group all minor links and footnotes at the bottom of a section, not in the main text. Phrase important links in this manner: *Watch out for misplaced modifiers—dangling, wandering, and squinting—that create unwittingly humorous descriptions.*

One of the best resources for intelligent online design is still the classic *Guide to Web Style* by Rick Levine, published by Sun Microsystems. See the Resources for Continuing Education appendix of this book for others.

If users can zero in on the questions they need answered by using keyword searches or creating bookmarks to the topics that perennially trouble them, they'll be less likely to "wing it" or "go by ear," two great ways to sabotage a style guide. And what an online style can do that even the best-indexed paper version can't is offer rapid and comprehensive searching and cross-referencing.

As the *Yale Style Guide* puts it, an intranet should let you "get in, get what you want, and move on." The section on intranet site design will be useful for any editor who is not familiar with the principles of online usability and navigation; here's the gist: "Successful intranet sites assemble *useful* information, organize it into *logical* systems, and deliver the information in an *efficient* manner" [emphasis ours]. For more, go to http://info.med.yale.edu/caim/manual/sites/intranet_design.html.

Time is money, especially when employees are trying to find an answer so they can get back to work. The single most important aspect to keep in mind when creating content for an online guide is the user. Providing navigation from place to place and interactive links within pages will help users get a sense of "you are here," without which "over there" may seem irrelevant instead of enriching.

A good overview of intranets in general—how and why to set them up and what the benefits, obstacles, and system requirements are—can be found at intranetroadmap.com, where an intranet service provider has provided an Intranet Road Map. A statistic quoted on the site: "Two-thirds of Fortune 1000 companies had an intranet as long ago as July 1996, according to the site, but who knows how many contained a companywide style guide. In our experience, some surprisingly high-profile, respected organizations and companies are winging it when it comes to quality control—or making arbitrary decisions that change with each new guard."

The truth is, online style guides don't rank high in the mind of anyone who isn't engaged in quality control of publications. But for those of us charged with saving organizational face and trying hard not to reinvent the wheel each time we edit a document, they're essential,

The *Yale Style Guide* says, "Graphic user interfaces were designed to give people direct control over their personal computers.... The goal is to provide for the needs of all your potential users, adapting Web technology to their expectations, and never requiring the readers to simply conform to an interface that puts unnecessary obstacles in their paths."

Here's a summary of what an efficient intranet site tries to do to speed users through the search and skim processes basic to consulting a style guide:

- Provide menus; tables of contents; button bars that let users go back, forward, or return to the opening page or a related menu page; and short summaries of what can be found on other pages. In short, give people who search differently a choice of paths leading to the same information.
- Highlight keywords, write meaningful heads and subheads, and incorporate a limited number of relevant links. (Too many links discourage users; irrelevant links infuriate them.)
- Be concise, organize information into short paragraphs, and don't use a line length the entire width of the screen. (On most monitors, there is a little bit of the "page" that a user can't see. Make sure vital information appears in the upper half of the screen.)
- Use hypertext links to accommodate the needs of many different users working on different types of publications for different media. Links will lead users to relevant pages for their particular project and allow them to bypass the rest, avoiding a sense of "too much information."

Reality: They're Going to Print Out Pages

Face it: Most people want a cheat sheet for the problems they encounter most often. Online pages containing a lot of text should be designed for printing (i.e., not extra-wide), because that's what people do with important online information—they want to have it on hand to absorb and refer to. You don't want users to lose a couple words off the right margin of the printed page. The recommended online page layout "safe area" dimensions for printing (from the *Yale Style Guide*) for a 640- by 480-pixel screen are 535 by 295.

If these basic ideas are new conceptual territory for you, it's time to have a meeting with your favorite resident programmer or webmaster to explain the scope and use of the guide you have in mind and to ask for help. Before you begin compiling content, think about how it must be organized for searching and linking, and learn enough about screen design to avoid simply parking a print piece online and failing to take advantage of interactivity and navigation tools.

DESIGN AND ACCESSIBILITY CONSIDERATIONS

You have to learn a bit about online design in order to write design-style guidance for your Web documents (or to edit them intelligently), as well as to help publish user-friendly online style guides.

According to the *Yale Style Guide*, readers see pages and screens first as a blur of shapes, text blocks, and color. Then they begin to pick out pieces of information. Type and illustration can help or can clutter the landscape with even more cues that are hard for readers to process. Hierarchy still matters very much online, but you won't necessarily achieve it by using the same physical cues you would in a printed reference. Adapted from the Yale guide, a checklist for enhancing readability:

- Direct the reader's eye toward important information right away with strong type.
- Use subtle pastel shades for background.
- Avoid bold, saturated colors except for accent or infrequent spots of emphasis.
- Make sure type contrasts sharply against any background color. Black type is best; reversed white type on a dark background can be hard to read.
- Beware of graphic embellishments you might use reflexively on paper— horizontal rules, bullets, icons, large display type sizes. They may look grotesque on your reader's browser.

The purpose of online design is to create a consistent, recognizable, simple plan whereby important elements look the strongest and content categories are logically organized and predictably flagged. (Don't make users guess when an underline is a live link and when it's an underline.)

We ask our readers to trust us when they see a link to another screenful of information. Will it be relevant, or just a slow-loading graphic? Will they find a useful design template or example sentences at the other end?

We need to use functional cues to help users understand how information is organized and how much attention they should give to certain parts in order to get to what they need. The *Yale Style Guide* unequivocally states that editorial landmarks like titles and headers are the fundamental human interface issue in Web pages, just as they are in any print publication. A consistent approach to titles, headlines, and subheads in your document will help your readers navigate through a complex set of Web pages.

Organizing a useful online reference actually requires that you create a style guide for the style guide! But that's not a problem—it's a chance to reinforce the guidelines by showing them at work. Decisions about using text styles consistently and emphatically in an intranet style guide might result in the following specs—which, ideally, would reflect the recommendations in the corporate style guide:

Headline style

Bold, capitalize initial letters—for document titles, other Web sites, proper names, product names, trade names

Downstyle

Bold, capitalize first word only—for subheads, references to other headings within the style manual, figure titles, lists

ROLLING OUT A STYLE GUIDE

The method you choose to introduce the style guide to your organization can significantly affect its success. You want your colleagues to regard the guide as an essential tool, not just another corporate manual that sits on the shelf (or on the intranet, as the case may be). When the guide is finally ready to be released and you are planning its distribution, consider the following approaches:

- Get buy-in from the top. Ask the CEO to sign a letter that discusses the organization's commitment to quality and the style guide's role in ensuring that the organization's written products—whether printed or electronic—represent it well. The overall message should be that everyone shares responsibility for upholding the organization's quality standards.
- Invite the users to a kickoff party. Give a presentation in which you explain how the guide is organized and how it should be used, but add an element of fun as well. One organization launched its guide with a contest, presented game-show-style, in which teams of participants scored points by answering questions about the company's editorial and design standards. (Wheee! We nerds sure know how to have fun, don't we?)
- Make it easy for people to ask questions. Although your ultimate goal is for people to use the guide rather than picking up the phone, give them a human point of contact (not just an e-mail box) to help them become familiar with the details. If a number of people have trouble with a particular section, you'll know what to focus on when you update the guide.

Here's a brief Q&A with director of publications Henry Dunbar, who recently led Reading Is Fundamental in the development and rollout of its corporate style guide:

Why did you decide you needed a new style guide? Who are its intended users? When I started to work at Reading Is Fundamental in 2000, we had no consistent way of editing printed or Web-based documents. We had different methods and habits in different departments, and differences within departments. There were AP- and Chicago-style disciples and a few MLA types, but the majority followed no style guide at all. They just wrote what they thought was grammatically correct. The intended users for the editorial style guide were all staff at our headquarters in Washington, DC (approximately 100 people). We weren't trying to establish editorial style guideline for the 4,100 people who run our programs nationwide, though we do provide them with logo usage guidelines.

What did you hope to accomplish with the guide—and have you seen evidence that the guide will support that? We hoped to make people aware of the need for editorial consistency, then to get them to follow the guidelines. Most staff people appreciate having the guide and make an effort to follow it. I base that assessment on the fact that I get questions periodically when people can't find the answers they seek. That means they are looking things up—they are using it. Obviously, I welcome their questions.

How is your guide made available? We provide all new staff with a paper version and have a PDF version on our internal network.

What were the hardest aspects for you in getting the guide compiled? Limiting the scope of the project was difficult—and wrapping it all up. Senior management supported our efforts, but then kept asking for additional sections to be added, such as guidelines for e-mail communication and fax cover sheets. We added them, but they were not in the original plan. We also have several "still to come" appendixes at the end because we wanted to get the most important sections distributed as soon as we had them.

What does your guide cover? Here is our TOC:

PART 1: INTRODUCTION
　A. Why Does RIF Have a Style Guide?
　B. Base Style Guide and Dictionaries

PART 2: WORDS

A. Frequently Used Terms

B. Acronyms, Abbreviations, and Titles

C. Common Grammar and Usage Problems

PART 3: STYLE AND FORMAT

A. Lists

B. Numbers

C. Citations and References

D. Capitalization

E. Common Punctuation Errors

F. Setting Off Words and Other Text

PART 4: PUBLICATIONS GUIDELINES

A. RIF Logo Usage

B. Trademarks and Copyrights

C. RIF Boilerplate and Mission and Vision Statements

D. Photo Releases

E. Press Releases

PART 5: INDIVIDUAL COMMUNICATION FORMAT

A. Correspondence

B. E-mail Communication

C. Fax Cover Sheets

PART 6: RIF PUBLICATIONS PROCESS

PART 7: FURTHER REFERENCE

APPENDICES (still to come)

A. Riffington

B. Cultural Sensitivity

C. Foreign Language Materials

D. Editing Checklist and Sample Writer's Guidelines

Can you share with us an excerpt from your instructions to users about why you hope they will use the guide and how you expect them to use it? Here is the text from the introduction:

> Editorial style is the uniform way in which the organization presents written information. Consistent presentation is important for any organization that

wants to project a professional image; it is vital to organizations that promote literacy. Having a consistent editorial style is a subtle but important way to tell the public that we care about how we communicate, and that we want our messages to be credible and accessible. Inconsistencies distract readers from the point of the communication. Additionally, having a set of predetermined guidelines saves everyone time, energy, and frustration.

As much as is possible, ALL written materials should adhere to this style. This includes:

- Printed publications (handbooks, brochures, newsletters, white papers, one-page briefs, collateral materials, technical assistance, etc.)
- Website information and electronic newsletters
- Press releases
- Executive briefings
- Presentations (including external PowerPoint presentations)
- Correspondence (including e-mail, letters, and faxes)

Exceptions can be made for specific projects and publications with the approval of the RIF Marketing and External Relations department.

Can you share with us an excerpt from the guide that illustrates some terms or usages special to RIF, which deviate from at least some other main style guides or dictionaries? This is the first page from our Frequently Used Terms section:

501(c)(3) No spaces between characters and parentheses. Microsoft Word may automatically turn the (c) into a circled copyright mark, so backspace to revert to parentheses. 501(c)(3) is a section of the Internal Revenue Code that designates an organization as charitable and tax exempt. Common usage: RIF is a *501(c)(3)*.

877-RIF-READ See style for **telephone numbers (Part 3B)**.

ABC-C Average book cost per child. Refers to a RIF program's budget divided by the number of children served with a 10 percent cushion factored in. Never use this abbreviation on documents and correspondence outside of the RIF office without defining it.

Adobe Acrobat A file reader that decodes documents to portable document format (PDF).

after-school, after school Hyphenate when used as an adjective (*after-school* activities, *after-school* programs). Otherwise, two words (He played with his friend *after school*).

age Use figures.

He is *5 years old*.
He will be *4* tomorrow.
The boy, *7*, has a sister, *10*.
Her daughter is *3 months old*.
The program is for children *ages 3 to 8*.
The activity is for children *ages 5 and up*.
She is in her *40s*. (no apostrophe)
Exception: 12 ten-year-olds, not 12 10-year-olds.

When age is expressed as an adjective before a noun or as a substitute for a noun, use hyphens.

A *5-year-old* boy.
It is for *8-year-olds*.

See general guidelines for **numbers (Part 3B)**. See also **grade level**.

age level Do not use this term. See **grade level**.

amended subcontract agreement Always lowercase. An amended subcontract agreement is issued if the program specialist and the local program coordinator determine that it is necessary to make changes to a proposal.

Anne Hazard Richardson RIF Volunteer of the Year Awards
First Reference: Always spell out and include *RIF* after *Anne Richardson* and before *Volunteer of the Year Awards*.
Subsequent References: *VOYA, RIF Volunteer of the Year Awards*, or *Volunteer of the Year Awards* is acceptable. *VOYA* can also refer to a person who receives the award. The VOYA program encourages local RIF programs to nominate an exceptional volunteer from their program for the award. One winner from each of the five RIF regions is selected and recognized.

approval packet Always lowercase. Packet mailed to local RIF program by national RIF once the local program's contract has been approved for the upcoming year. It contains the subcontract agreement signed by a RIF official, a blank performance report, distribution reports, ledger, and Invoice Verification Form, as well as the approval letter, any other necessary letters, and any technical assistance materials requested by the RIF program. See **IVF**.

at risk, at-risk Only use hyphen when the term is used as an adjective. Preferred: Children who are *at risk* of educational failure. Acceptable, but try to avoid: RIF serves *at-risk* children in every state.

Authorizing Official Always capitalize. Always define at first reference. An Authorizing Official (AO) is the person with the highest authority at the local organization operating a RIF program. For example, the Authorizing Official for a school with a RIF program is the principal. Acceptable to abbreviate as *AO* after first reference.

board of directors Lowercase.
First Reference: Always write out board of directors or the complete name of the board. (Carol Rasco serves on RIF's *board of directors*.)
Subsequent References: Acceptable to use only *board*. (She has been on the *board* for three years.) Exception: Board or board of directors can be capitalized if used as a title that precedes a name. See **Part 3D** for more rules about capitalizing titles.

Does RIF have a separate set of guidelines for its Web site? Do the print and Web people have a cooperative QC process before new content that is being published goes live? Or are they separate teams, and corrections get made after the fact (as is so common)? The website is supposed to follow the style guide. Current staff people make every effort to comply, but whole sections of the site were created before the style guide existed. Going back and updating those pages has been a slow process. This is primarily due to the fact that the web team's priority is for getting new content up. They are a separate editorial team and have their own QC process. [Note: RIF styles these terms *website* and *web*.]

What is the main way you get people to pay attention to the style guide? They are introduced to it at a new staff orientation and corrected when examples of incorrect style are found. We have toyed with the idea of sending weekly examples of correct and incorrect style, but haven't implemented this of yet. For the most part, people are eager to use it and find it helpful. Oddly, while this is designed for RIF purposes, many staff take the guide with them when they leave or ask for a copy when they get to their new jobs.

What other central guides and dictionaries do you refer staff to for additional guidance, whether printed or online? Again, from the Introduction:

> The *RIF Style Guide and Publications Manual* is not meant to be comprehensive, but it should cover most issues concerning printed publications. Please use this as a primary resource when addressing editorial concerns. A style committee will review the guide periodically and make additions and changes as necessary. Decisions will be made based on what best serves the organization. For issues and topics not covered in the *RIF Style Guide*, please consult these guides (in this order):

Associated Press Stylebook and Libel Manual (RIF's base guide)
Chicago Manual of Style (15th edition)
New York Public Library Writer's Guide to Style and Usage

Additionally, any modern dictionary can be used as a reference for spelling, but when disputes or inconsistencies arise, the RIF publications team will use the online dictionary at www.m-w.com as the final authority. This is for cost and access reasons.

Questions about this guide may be referred to the RIF director of publications.

UPDATING YOUR STYLE GUIDE

Depending on the speed with which technical terminology changes and professional information becomes obsolete in a particular field, realistically, any style guide will probably be slightly out of date to some degree the minute it is released. The question is, how often do *significant* changes occur that affect the usefulness and credibility of the guide?

For a technology-oriented company, that might be once a month, because product names and version numbers are key elements of corporate documentation. For an association, annual updates might be sufficient. The job of maintaining the style guide can take on a life of its own if its contents are not monitored by someone with a sense of proportion about the importance of changes.

Updating the style guide gives an organization the opportunity to ask itself the all-important question "Why do we do it this way?" The process of documenting decisions can highlight standards that have become obsolete. Sometimes specifications can be traced to old technology (maybe the requirement to produce all presentations in Helvetica started because that was the only typeface available on the network printer in 1992). Make the most of updating by questioning old practices and changing those that no longer make sense.

Here is one approach for managing the update process:

- Once the style guide has been distributed, designate someone to be the collection point for questions. Include a feedback mechanism (a short, simple printed or electronic form) with the guide to make it easy for people to offer comments.
- Decide whether you will update the guide frequently to incorporate minor revisions (and call it Version 1.1) or less frequently to incorporate major changes (and call it Version 2.0).
- Define the review process. Minor updates might require the eyes of only a few reviewers; major updates should be routed to the entire development committee, and probably to a sampling of users.

- For minor updates, indicate what changed (either with a cover memo or by inserting change bars in the margins) and redistribute the guide. For major updates, consider convening the users for a presentation of the changes. Major changes should include some discussion—whether at the presentation or in the guide itself—of the rationale behind them or an explanation of why an exception to conventional wisdom is being made. Users will be far more likely to change their ways if they understand why they are being asked to take a different approach.

GUIDANCE FOR WEB SITES, TOO

Web sites need a consistent style to guide their content providers and maintenance staff. A dynamic site tends to grow quickly as new kinds and levels of information about products, services, references, and people are added. New content shouldn't be added without regard for consistent style across pages, which will also make updating the site easier. HTML formatting tags can be done several ways; pick one way and stick with it to avoid erratic formatting.

As Web sites proliferate, a primary style task is to integrate the distinctive elements that tell visitors they're visiting *your* site. Controls should work the same on every page; backgrounds, section colors, the name of your organization, addresses, logo treatment, trademark symbols, copyright statements—all of it should be coordinated. Make sure your guide advises against using browser-specific design elements that detract from the information mission. Each Web page should be proofread before it goes to the site, and the chain-of-approval process should be clear. If more than one person works on the site, designate who can authorize exceptions to the style and in what cases.

THE REALITY OF GATEKEEPING

One final bit of advice: No matter how careful you are to make your style guide easy to understand and a good thing to use, a few people will always simply ignore it. These are the same people who don't read their employee P&P manual and wonder why they are suddenly out of leave. Don't think of them as either your target audience or The Enemy. The real target audience for guidance is everyone who—though perhaps not publication specialists by training—wants the written products their hands touch to be clear, useful, and produced in an efficient manner. We'd be willing to bet that most of the people in your organization fall into this category. Best to act as if you believe so and approach your role of gatekeeper with optimism, assuming the best of everyone. Even the renegade in IT who refuses to recognize that the series comma is his style, too, because no mandate is an island when it comes to Our Style.

10

New Usage: Adventuresome, Troublesome, or Tiresome?

The folks who toil in the trenches writing code or developing new hardware don't mind being called geeks; it's a badge of honor. Nor do they flinch at the jargon that identifies them as insiders and bewilders us outsiders—that's one of the functions of jargon. When you encounter geekspeak, pause for a moment. Can you provide enough context to guide your readers to its meaning without plain-Englishing the flavor and exactitude out of it? If you can, please do.

If you were writing about any niche—cowhands, Marines, politicians—you wouldn't purge their speech of anything that wasn't standard English. Rather, you would use their idiosyncratic vocabulary to give a vivid picture of their work.

The fact is that we've all picked up more tech terms than we probably realize from accumulated years of exposure to computers, digital music and TV, the Web, e-mail, and other aspects of the wired life.

Many tech-offshoot terms have become mainstreamed so smoothly that we don't hear them as jargon any longer. When the first edition of this book came out, *offline* was defined as "disconnected and unable to receive data," "the noncomputerized world," or, informally, "time spent away from computers and the Internet, and unreachable by e-mail." Now *going offline* can mean shutting down a Web site or server for temporary maintenance, or discontinuing a blog or online business for good. We've also heard it used jokingly to mean "going on vacation" and "leaving work."

But how, when you're not personally familiar with the terms, can you tell the difference between true jargon that needs editing and acceptable idiomatic expressions? Well, if you see that a word contains recognizable parts of other familiar words (*cognates*), you're probably safe to leave the term to stand on its own in context. For example, people are likely to understand that *infotainment* has something to do with both news and entertainment. But what about *webrary?* You may not think it sounds euphonious, but it would be silly to place an explanatory "Web library" in parentheses for most audiences.

Along with every other industry, print publishing—traditionally somewhat conservative and not terribly fond of technology for its own sake—has been waffling when it comes to "allowing" new terms and the more contemporary forms of evolving terms. Frankly, many Internet publishers are more interested in how well graphics, links, and information architecture work than in whether their Web content contains erratic, contradictory spellings like *policymaking, policy-makers,* and *policy driven.*

Somewhere between the editorially conservative and radically unruly zones is where most of us are trying to strike a balance. Guess what? That's more work than either extreme. Of course you'll want to ensure the integrity of the text. Ignoring mechanical inconsistencies signals carelessness or a lack of professional savvy that may be symptomatic of more substantial errors of fact, logic, and analysis. Rein in the "clean-up reflex" when it comes to new terms until you've researched them and are certain there's a better way to express the ideas they're trying to convey.

With so much usage in flux, a rigid insistence on old-fashioned style is neither necessary nor advisable—as, for example, always revising new *-ize* terms like *incentivize* and "nouned" verbs like *transition* and *grow.*

Some usages are now widely acceptable but still controversial. For example, some editors swear that never on their watch will a writer get away with the third-person plural pronoun to refer inclusively to both genders—as in this example: *Each editor must make **their** own decision about the relative merits of bias-free language, terms of art, and strict grammaticality.* Other editors allow the "singular their" as a smoother workaround than "his or her." The point is to keep up acceptable alternatives rather than trying to enforce hard-and-fast rules.

YOUR BEST GUESS MIGHT BE "THE AUTHORITY"

Perhaps the biggest challenge is the variant forms on their way to convergence sooner or later, one way or another. When you have to choose among alternative forms, someone will think you're wrong no matter what you decide.

The names of charities, nonprofits, and government agencies, bureaus, and departments contain old-fashioned spellings that can't be easily changed, but the publications professionals who work for them try to use updated spellings in their content, even if those spellings don't match the formal, legally mandated name. So be it; editorial consistency is a goal—but almost nowhere is it achieved 100 percent.

Webster's Collegiate lists *fundraising* as a solid term, so when the chief professional organization of fundraisers was poised for a stem-to-stern repositioning, including a new name, a new spelling could be justified as in keeping with contemporary style. The organization's acronym went from NSFRE (National Society of *Fund Raising* Executives—with a hyphen as an adjective in text but not in the official name) to AFP (Association of *Fundraising* Professionals).

Of course, when AFP's magazine and Web site are referring to literature of the field from all over the globe, *fundraising*, *fund raising*, and *fund-raising* will still be all over the place; retroactive editing of the spelling of evolving words in previously published documents isn't acceptable or feasible.

Publications that report news are in a similar fix; for example, dictionaries report that the consensus is to spell *airline* solid. But a quote attributed to a spokesperson from the Air Line Pilots Association (in the same *Washington Post* article that mentions the Airline Pilots Security Alliance) ignores that guidance. Further, ALPA's acronym would become APA if it were updated for the spelling of *airline*—and there are already lots of APAs, so the discrepancy is probably an enduring fact of life.

This phenomenon is what EEI Press editors call *perceived inconsistency.* Someone is making conscientious editorial decisions that may, however, look like inconsistent treatments. The cure for this is a fatalistic shrug and a note in your style guide about such deliberate departures from contemporary style.

And as the new gets old, some older, simpler terms may start looking better and better. We have to keep watching new-media terms to see whether they're "nonce" terms—just for now—or have legs and will end up in dictionaries. Now that we've all heard about *repurposing* content, some of us wonder why we don't flag that word as tedious jargon for *reusing*, *recycling*, or the more accurate *multipurposing*. We've already mentioned the *extreme* (as in *Extreme Home Makeover*) school of hype. More commonly, the prefixes *e*, *i*, and *cyber* are overused in farfetched coinages: *e-prayer*, *iSuccess-zine*, *cyberrific.*

The one thing you can count on is the steady evolution toward *down style*, a trend toward omitting optional but unnecessary and possibly intrusive capitalization and punctuation. You'll find a related discussion in the *Chicago Manual of Style*'s distinction between open (omitting discretionary commas) and closed punctuation. But the point of down style is not the abandonment of rules; it is to simplify what is already correct on the premise that even simpler is even better—more readily accessible to readers.

Here are the types of terms that you need to keep an eye on, look up in one of the major or specialized dictionaries, make decisions about, and add to your proprietary style guide. Make it a habit to check with the "Words to Watch" list on the eeicom.com/press/istyle companion site for this book. Recommendations and observations on evolving usage and new jargon, pooled by EEI Press editors, will give you a starting point. But realize that, when major authorities disagree, the best you can do is choose the style most consonant with your main style guide and most likely to suit your audience.

WORDS TO KEEP AN EYE ON

These are the main categories into which editorial challenges fall:

- Terms with idiosyncratic spelling for which all mnemonics fail. You'll probably have to look up *eBay* so you can get it right for an article you're writing about online auction sites—and remember to capitalize it when it starts a sentence.
- Preferred, acceptable, evolving, and problematic usage of new terms as nouns, verbs, and modifiers. You don't want to be one of those people with pursed lips rapping the knuckles of your coworkers for saying "E-mail me" instead of "Send me an e-mail note," do you? Or will you cheer them on to all sorts of *e*-verbs such as *e-leverage*? Decide where the comfort zone is for you and your organization on the spectrum of innovative terms.
- Terms with arbitrary style treatments, including commonly used abbreviations, acronyms, and initialisms. A good number of new-media words, especially prefixed by the notorious, glorious *e, i,* and *cyber* words, are coined for marketing purposes or are proprietary names and trademarks. Record the ones you use most often. Accept that complete consistency is impossible.
- Terms that are best left unchanged—even if they strike you as too informal or jargonish—as long as they are clear in context. It marks you as old-fashioned to try to turn every Web- and computing-related idiom into quasi-formal English. Many words on the fringe as we write this guide will become household words before long.
- When corporate publications, marketing materials, and Web content contain a lot of special terms and reflect the style preferences of many different authors, it's important to create and enforce an in-house style guide. Key areas in which to make consistent decisions include capitalization, punctuation, spelling, and preferred usage for enforcing trademarks and other proprietary names.

For example, one of your guidelines might be "Don't use *e-mousetraps* as generic shorthand; use *eMousetrap rodent control devices*." (By the way, when we wrote that mousetrap example, it was imaginary. But just to be safe, we did a search and discovered that it's indeed a trademark. Scary how thin the dividing line has become between the real and the theoretical.)

When in doubt, look for precedents. Trust yourself to intervene (or not) as called for when you can't find them. And once you've made a decision, record it so you don't have to go through the same song-and-dance again.

Here's a selection of tech terms that have become common—in some cases, too common. Keep on eye on how they're being used, and you'll glean some facts about the computing and online world that will help you sound a less fractious alarm the next time you're confronted with geekspeak (which can be actually be pretty clever).

24/7 (adj., adv.) Used to indicate a service or source that's available around the clock, 24 hours a day, seven days a week—usually via the Internet. "Our customer service department is open *24/7* to serve you." Also written *24-7, 24 x 7* and—awkwardly—*twenty-four seven* (the "Tina Turner *Twenty-Four Seven* Millennium Tour"). **Note:** This is just a jauntier way of saying "Open 24 hours" and "Open All Night," and it connotes online availability rather than a pharmacy or coffee shop.

access (n.) To have or gain access refers to the privilege or right to use a computer resource. "All employees have *access* to the company intranet." (v.) *To access* means to be able to gain access to data, a system, or processes. **Note:** Many conservative editors consider the verb *access* jargon in need of a specific translation: "She couldn't *access* the extra key" means she couldn't *find* it.

accessible (adj.) *Accessible* features and operating controls have been designed for easy use by people with disabilities (visual, physical, or mental impairments): *wheelchair-accessible*. In a new-media context, *accessible* may also describe the degree to which features can be taken advantage of by nonnative English speakers and Internet users from developing countries who have very slow dial-up speeds. In these senses, accessible has become a euphemism.

analog (adj.) New-technology writing often uses the contrasting terms *analog* and *digital*. Most of creation breaks down into either analog or digital, and as the world sweeps toward an increasingly digital age, it is important to know the difference. *Analog* processes represent data as variables that vary continuously rather than discretely. *Digital* processes are represented by numerical values—at the most basic, 1 or 0 (for on or off). They also represent a finite number of values. For example, a *digital watch* display leaps from one number to the next; it displays a finite number of variables (times of the day). In contrast, an *analog watch* (the old-fashioned kind with hands that move) represents an infinite number of variables as its hands sweep around the dial. Most modern computers are *digital*; human beings are *analog*.

analog-to-digital converter (ADC) (n.) Hyphenated. Also called an *A-D* or *A-to-D converter*. Watch the news for this acronym in the run-up to 2008's mandated conversion of analog TV signals to digital-only.

authoring (v.) To *author* still means to write an article or a book, but it has the new-media connotation of creating an online application such as a multimedia presentation, help system, or computer-based training program. (adj.) *Authoring tools, authoring system, authoring language, authoring program.*

B2B (adj.) Short for *business-to-business,* meaning business that is transacted between businesses, rather than from business to consumer. This abbreviation is also seen as b-to-b and B-to-B. Related: B2C (business-to-consumer) and P2P (peer-to-peer).

bricks-and-mortar (adj.) In cyber-jargon, *bricks-and-mortar* (also seen as *brick-and-mortar*) refers to business conducted in a physical office, building, or retail store, as opposed to an operation existing exclusively on the Web, which is called a *clicks-and-mortar* store—see that entry. These terms are dated, and many businesses have both an online and a land presence.

cellular phone (n.) Synonyms include *cell phone, cellular telephone, digital phone, mobile phone,* and *cell. Cell phone* is commonly accepted; *cellular telephone* is overly formal for most contexts.

clicks-and-mortar (adj.) *Clicks-and-mortar* is a play on bricks-and-mortar. A *bricks-and-mortar* store has a tangible physical presence, as opposed to a store operating totally online. *Clicks-and-mortar* has most often been used to refer to businesses that have both an online and a physical (storefront) business presence. But it's also used to describe retail stores that feature Web kiosks and make Web site transactions available to customers while they're physically in the store. "Clicks-and-mortar companies offer consumers several options for merchandise returns."

clickstream (n.) The pattern of mouse clicks a user makes while working on a computer or navigating through sites on the Web. The *clickstream* shows, for example, the path the user took to navigate through a Web site or between Web sites. **Note:** Follows the pattern for *mainstream* and *downstream.*

clickthrough (n.) *Clickthrough* is a Web advertising term for when a person clicks on an Internet banner ad and triggers the associated hyperlink that leads to more information. (adj.) The *clickthrough rate* refers to the percentage of viewers of a Web banner ad who clicked on the ad. **Note:** Follows the pattern set by clickstream, but creates a perceived inconsistency if your style is followthrough rather than *followthrough.*

co-locate (v.) In the wired world, to *co-locate* one's Web server means to locate it physically on another company's Internet-connected network. (n.) *co-location*. (adj.) *a co-location facility, co-location service.* Sometimes spelled *colocate* or *colocation*. This word is frequently misspelled as *collocation*, which means to place or group together. **Note:** Look both spellings up in a dictionary to see how confusing such distinctions can be for style-guide users. That's why specific examples are so helpful in a guide.

content forward (n.)The philosophy that the editorial mission of a Web site—the audience it serves and the types of content delivered—should drive the graphic design and functionality built into the site. Too often, design and technical functionality are used as substitutes for meeting audience expectations. Making a site pretty, fast, and full of gee-whiz technology should never be a substitute for making it timely, topical, and persistently relevant. Meaningful content truly is what people seek and what technology serves but cannot alone provide.

convergence (n.) In the realm of information technology, *convergence* refers to the combining of computer, communications, and consumer electronics technologies. (adj.) A good example of *convergent technology* is a cell phone with information-sharing features like a GPS, Internet access, instant messaging, and a camera.

cross-post (v.) To *cross-post* means to post the same message to several different newsgroups or mailing lists at about the same time.

cyber- words (n., v.) Originally from *cybernetics*, the cut form *cyber* is usually attached to words to add the cachet of being computerized, electronic, or Internet-based. Most *cyber-* terms are closed compounds such as *cyberbuck, cybercafe, cybercash, cybercommerce, cyberculture, cybercop, cyberfeminism, cyberlawyer, cybernaut, cyberpiracy, cybersex, cyberspace, cybersquat, cybersurfer, cyberworld*. At times, open compounds are clearer and more attractive: *cyber economy, cyber investor.*

data (n.) In purely statistical or scientific usage, *data* is a plural (or count) noun meaning "pieces of information." *Datum* is the singular. But *data* is widely and increasingly acceptable in a collective (or mass noun rather than count noun) sense used with a singular verb. That's using *data* journalistically to mean "cumulative bits of information." When *data* means "information stored electronically," we recommend using *data* in its singular sense, with a singular verb: "The *data was* restored from the backup disk." Certainly we would say, "The *data is* corrupt" rather than "The *data are* corrupt," unless we are statisticians.

data- Compounds formed from the word *data* are almost always open or hyphenated, whether used as nouns, verbs, or adjectives: *data bank, data bit, data bus, data center, data-driven processing, data entry, data field, data file, data flow, data link, data mart, data mining, data offset, data packet, data point, data rate, data set, data sink, data stream, data warehouse.* Notable exceptions are *database, database administrator, database engine, datacom, datagram.*

desktop (n.) 1. In a GUI, the *desktop* is the computer's onscreen work area, where icons and menus allow the user to access all programs and functions. Also called an *electronic desktop.* 2. *Jargon.* A *desktop* is also a computer that is small enough to fit on top of a desk or in a person's work area, short for *desktop computer* or *desktop model computer.* (adj.) 1. Pertaining to the GUI desktop: *desktop level.* For example, "All the programs and functions on a computer can be accessed from the desktop level." 2. Activities and technology designed to be accessible from the user's business desk: *desktop computer, desktop conferencing, desktop publishing, desktop video.*

digerati (n.) A play on the Italian word *literati, digerati* refers to the elite of the digital revolution. (If you're not among them, are you one of the dig-illiterati?)

digi- words *Jargon. Digi-* words are compounds derived from digital. They are generally spelled as closed compounds. For example: *digibabble, digispeak, digitocracy, digerati.*

digital (adj.) As an adjective, *digital* adds the loose connotation that something is used on a computer or is computerized. Examples are *digital cash, digital certificate, digital money, digital network, digital photography, digital recording, digital signature, digital video.* For a comparison of digital and analog processes, see analog.

digitize (v.) To convert an image, text, or signal into digital code using a scanner or converter. "The 16 mm film of Kennedy's assassination was *digitized* by the National Archives."

disc, disk (n.) *Disc* is an alternative spelling for *disk.* The storage medium determines the correct spelling to use. Most authorities agree that *magnetic computer disks* are generally spelled with a *k* (*floppy disk, hard disk, magneto-optical disk, RAM disk, diskette*) and *optical disks* with a *c* (*video disc, compact disc, laser disc, digital versatile disc*). However, a number of the sources we reviewed did not distinguish between *disc* and *disk.* From our review, it seems premature to blur the lines that far. Perhaps the easiest generalization that will serve most writers and editors is that CDs are *discs* and all other types of storage media are *disks*. (adj.) *disk drive, disk farm, disk mirroring, disk operating system* (DOS), *disk partition.*

disintermediation (n.) This means "the elimination of the middleman." One of the theories about how Web commerce will change the world is that it will lead to the *disintermediation* of retail sales. However, as anyone who has ever had an online order form or process go awry knows, customer service still matters to online consumers. On a TV news program profiling Netflix, the CEO ran into a problem in a demo and could not find an 800 telephone number anywhere on the Web site for live human help—an oversight that was quickly rectified. The editors of this book believe access to intermediaries is Business 101.

download (v.) It means to receive data from a remote computer over a network or Internet connection. (n.) *Download* is also used as a noun: "Our Web site features a free *download* for people who register." This use verges on jargon, although it has become increasingly common. For now, we recommend recasting the sentence; for example: "People who register on our Web site can *download* a free electronic publication." Be aware of the difference between *download* and *upload*. A file is *downloaded* when it is received from a remote location. You *upload* a file when you transmit it to a remote location.

drag and drop *Jargon.* We've seen this common computer expression used as a verb, adjective, and noun. (v.) While the expression "*drag and drop* the icon into the trashcan" hurts the ears, *drag and drop* clearly expresses an instruction for a specific action. In the *Microsoft Press Computer Dictionary* we find the following more palatable—if lengthier—example: "To delete a document in the Mac OS, a user can *drag* the document icon across the screen *and drop* it on the trashcan icon." A similar expression is click and drag. (adj.) When *drag and drop* is used as an adjectival compound, we hyphenate it, as in the sentence "Both the Windows and the Mac OS offer *drag-and-drop functionality.*" (n.) *Drag and drop* is also used as a noun. In the *Free Online Dictionary of Computing* we found the following example: "The biggest problem with *drag and drop* is does it mean 'copy' or 'move'?"

DTP *desktop publishing.* (n., adj.) The line between DTP and word processing has become moot as word processors acquire more sophisticated page layout features. The distinction we usually draw is that the purpose of *DTP* is to prepare professional publications for commercial printing. Word processors are well-suited to preparing documents for office laser printer output. At the low end, however, home *DTP packages* allow users to create nicely embellished publications like greeting cards and certificates for output to an inkjet printer.

At the high end, word processors can be used to produce books for commercial reproduction and binding on a DocuTech machine. (It may no longer be necessary in the publishing world to spell out *DTP* on first use, but it's a courtesy.) It's also advisable to begin a sentence with the spelled-out form (as for many other acronyms).

DVD *digital versatile disc.* (n.) Originally known as the *digital video disc*, this disc looks like a **CD-ROM** but holds much more data, which permits full-length movies and audio programs to be recorded on the disc. *DVD* refers to the disc itself. Also common is *DVD-ROM*—this is a read-only *DVD*. A *DVD* can be recorded on both sides and holds several gigabytes of data per side; new technology will increase the storage capacity to over eight gigabytes per side. The device that plays the *DVD* is called a *DVD drive* (or *DVD-ROM drive*) or *DVD device*. The newer *DVD devices* can play and record to both *DVDs* and CDs. (adj.) *DVD technology, DVD drive, DVD device, DVD player.*

DVD-R *digital versatile disc-recordable.* (n.) A write-once DVD.

DVD-RAM, DVD+RW (n.) Competing (and incompatible) standards for a high-capacity, rewritable DVD.

DVD-ROM *digital versatile disc-ROM.* (n.) A read-only DVD.

dynamic (adj., adv.) *Dynamic actions* take place when they are needed rather than in advance. *Dynamic Web pages* are composed of components collected and served on demand or on the fly. ASP (Active Server Pages) is one of several proprietary technologies that enable generation of *dynamically created pages.*

e- words The prefix *e-* is short for *electronic*. *E- words* are catchy, popular, and probably the most abused category of words in the English language today. Words like *e-commerce, e-business,* and *e-mail* have sprung from nowhere into the mainstream in a matter of years. Marketing copywriters, headline writers, and startup companies have turned just about every conceivable word into an *e-word* to give it the cachet of "modern, new, and electronic." Readers may regard new *e-words* as trite rather than clever; exercise restraint in coining them. For consistency, we prefer to spell *e-words* with a hyphen, and that includes *e-mail.*

e-book, eBook (n.) Strictly speaking, an *e-book* is an electronic book. But be aware when you use the word that the electronic publishing industry is swiftly redefining what exactly *e-book* means. The Open Electronic Book Forum has defined a common technical standard for the electronic book called the Open eBook Publication Structure Specification. Read more about this initiative at openebook.org. (adj.) To read an *e-book* usually requires an *e-book device* or *e-book reader.* A dedicated *e-book reader* is a handheld device designed for optimal *e-book viewing. Rocket eBook* is a trademark of NuvoMedia.

editor (n.) A program used to create and edit text and code: *a text editor, line editor, HTML editor, source code editor.* An *editor* is less powerful than a word (or text) processor, which in turn is less powerful than a desktop publishing (DTP) program. A word processor usually has much more sophisticated formatting features than an *editor.* Also a *video editor*—a machine used to edit video. (v.) *To edit, editing* (code, HTML, etc.). (n.) A person who *edits.* (v.) To prepare for publication or public presentation. To alter, adapt, or refine especially to bring about conformity to a standard or to suit a particular purpose— "carefully *edited* the speech" (from *Webster's 10th*). *Editors* are not mere rule appliers. In the electronic age, they are called on more and more to be arbiters of the language where style guides and clearly defined rules do not exist.

e-mail (n.) Short for electronic mail, *e-mail* used as a noun refers to both an electronic text message (*an e-mail*) and the system of communication by electronic text messages over a network (*communicating by e-mail*). (adj.) *E-mail message, e-mail system, e-mail traffic.* (v.) To send messages by *e-mail.* Less common spellings are *email* and *E-mail.* Use *E-mail* at the beginning of sentences. Use two initial caps for title case (E-Mail). We've drawn a line in the sand by specifying *e-mail* rather than *email.* The trend, especially among computer industry publications, is toward the closed form. However, because *e-mail* falls within the group we've classified as *e-words,* we prefer to treat it consistently with words of parallel construction. *Ecommerce* and *ebusiness* are not as widely used as *e-commerce* and *e-business,* so we recommend keeping the hyphen in *e-mail*—for now.

e-tailing *electronic retailing.* (n.) This word popped into prominence late in 1999 as the US financial and popular press closely monitored the performance of online merchants (e-tailers) during the Christmas season. (adj.) It has fallen into disuse.

extranet (n.) This is the portion of a corporate intranet that is available to customers/clients, vendors, suppliers, and/or business partners, usually employing password-protected access.

extreme *Jargon.* (adj.) Successor to *the bleeding edge.* Over the past several years, *extreme* has been used to mean "pushing the edge" or "taken to the ultimate extent" in many contexts—it's quickly becoming institutionalized as it is co-opted for marketing purposes. *Extreme sports* have lead to the *X-Games*. So *extreme* doesn't necessarily add the connotation of digital or electronic, although the Internet and all its associated technologies have pushed every-body to the *extreme edge* in one way or another (feeling *extreme* information anxiety anyone?). Anything that challenges the mind, imagination, or body is, idiomatically speaking, *extreme*. There will always be an *extreme edge*—maybe the word *extreme* won't be enough to describe it, though, as the hype inevitably becomes the norm, and then is demoted to the equivalent of merely clichéd, *extremely cool*.

e-zine See zine.

FAQ *Jargon.* (n.) A *FAQ* is a list of *frequently asked questions,* usually posted on a newsgroup or Web site to provide a place to answer common questions asked by newcomers. Use of *FAQ* outside the Web and newsgroup context has become trendy, but it should be used carefully—not everyone will know what you mean. (adj.) A *FAQ list.* Pronounced "F-A-Q" or "fack."

fax (n., v.) Only if you wish to be perceived as hopelessly out of it will you spell *facsimile* out or capitalize it as FAX. Frowned upon as jargon as recently as 10 years ago, *fax* is now perfectly acceptable as a transitive verb with an indirect object: *Fax me your resume.*

font (n.) The difference between a *font* and a *typeface* can be confusing. In brief, a *font* is a set of characters for a particular typeface. A *typeface* is a design for a set of characters. Among the most common business-document *typefaces* are Courier, Times Roman, and Helvetica. Each *typeface* is made up of sets of *fonts,* which describe characteristics such as size, weight, and slant. Most *typefaces* include a minimum of four *fonts:* normal weight, bold, italic, and bold italic. For links to typography resources and examples of contemporary fonts, visit philsfonts.com. (adj.) A *font family* is a complete set of fonts for the same typeface (usually includes normal weight, bold, italic, and bold italic fonts). *Font cartridge, font manager, font metric, font style, font utility, font weight.* For a look at fonts suitable for the Web, visit online foundries.

FTP *File Transfer Protocol.* (n.) An Internet-based method for transferring information from one computer to another. (v.) To upload or download files to/from another computer using File Transfer Protocol: *to FTP files, FTPed, FTPing.* (adj.) *An FTP site.* Use initial caps for the acronym although in an address it'll be lowercased. When writing an *FTP address* in text, include the prefix *ftp://,* as in *ftp://ftp.tradesvc.com/tsp/incoming/.* See also HTTP.

handheld (n.) A *handheld* usually refers to a computer that is small enough to fit in one hand. A *handheld* usually performs a number of functions and receives input from a keypad or device such as a pointer or barcode scanner. (adj.) *Handheld PC, handheld computer.* A palmtop is a type of handheld device.

hardcopy (n., adj.) Style it as one word. *Hardcopy* refers to the physical, paper version of a document or a printout of data as opposed to the electronic version, as in "I need the *hardcopy* as well as the electronic version." The opposite, *softcopy*, is not as common but refers to an electronic version.

HDML *handheld device markup language*

HDTV *high-definition television*

high-tech (adj.) Hyphenated as an adjective when it precedes the noun, and we propose it hyphenated as a unit modifier, too. Occasionally but not preferably seen as *hi-tech*.

hit (n.) A *hit* is an often-misunderstood Web site traffic statistic. Often the number of *hits* is taken to mean unique visitors or pageviews. However, a hit is the total number of files downloaded or accessed. One page may consist of several files, as the viewer of a page has access not only to the page itself but also to the graphics and any scripts running on that page. Therefore, one *pageview* may generate dozens of *hits*. This statistic is misleading when it's used to quantify a site's total traffic. A graphics-intensive site that receives a million *hits* a month may actually be receiving fewer unique visitors who are seeing fewer pageviews than another site that delivers fewer files.

home page (n.) The *home page* is the main page for a Web site. Spelled as two words, consistent with **Web page.** Every Web site has a home page; complex Web sites may have multiple *entry pages*—say, to feature specific products—but only one *home page.* The *home page* does not automatically mean the *opening screen.* Some sites use splash screens before the home page. An alternative, less common spelling is *homepage.*

HTML *Hypertext Markup Language*

HTTP *Hypertext Transfer Protocol.* (n.) HTTP is the basic protocol or standard that allows documents to be delivered across the Web. Any Web browser can communicate with a server using *HTTP.* The *http://* prefix in a Web address tells the Web browser that the document conforms to the *HTTP standard.* If the communications protocol is not specified, the browser assumes that it conforms to *HTTP.* Capitalize the acronym and use initial caps when spelling it out. See also FTP and URL.

hyper- words Most words using the prefix *hyper-* are written as closed compounds: *hyperlink, hypermedia, hyperspace, hypertext, hyperware,* but *hyper-reality.*

i- words *Jargon.* The *i-* prefix stands for Internet. *I*-words are spelled as hyphenated compounds (*i-content, i-publishing*) and also as closed compounds with an intercap to avoid pronunciation confusion (*iVillage.com, iPublish.com*).

inhouse (adj., adv.) One word. *Inhouse* work is performed within the company or organization as opposed to work that is *outsourced,* which is the opposite term.

instant message (IM) (n.) An *instant message* is a message sent from one computer to another over a network or the Internet that appears in real time. The acronym is now used almost universally as a verb: *to IM.* "We IM'd back and forth all afternoon." *IM, IMing, IM'd.* Also called *Internet chat.* The key distinction between *e-mail* and *instant messaging* is that *IMs* appear onscreen on the recipient's computer as soon as they are received; *e-mail* messages sit on a server until the recipient retrieves them.

Internet (n.) When referring to the worldwide network of computer networks that communicate with each other, the word *Internet* is always capitalized. (adj.) *Internet-based toy sales, Internet address.* The *Web* is just one part of the *Internet,* which also includes functions such as e-mail, FTP, Gopher, Telnet, and others.

intranet (n., adj.) Refers to a company's internal network of HTML pages. Do not shorten to *Net* or *net,* as this can be mistaken for a reference to *the Internet.* Refer to it as the corporation's *intranet site* (or *the intranet* on internal company documents). Do not refer to an intranet as a *Web* or *web.* Although they use the same technology, intranet sites are not on the Internet but rather are accessible from the company's network.

IT *information technology.* (n., adj.) This acronym is used loosely to refer to any and all tasks, skills, and activities associated with computers, the Web, and new media. The people in *IT departments* purchase, install, upgrade, and troubleshoot software, hardware, peripherals, and related electronic systems. *IT* may mean anything from database management and programming to daily maintenance of a network, applications support, and Web site development. The oldest synonym for *IT* is *MIS* (*management information systems*), which gradually gave way to the less-clunky *IS* (*information systems*). Now the broader term *IT* is most frequently seen. It seems that a boundless array of powerful, complementary technologies—which have forced even the stodgiest publisher onto the Internet—simply overtook the more static "system" model.

just-in-time (JIT) (n.) Just-in-time is hyphenated when it refers to the manufacturing and inventory management strategy. (adj.) Its most prominent tool is POD—print-on-demand technology.

LISTSERV (adj.) *LISTSERV* is a registered trademark for the **electronic mailing list** management software marketed by L-Soft. Be careful not to misuse *LISTSERV* as a synonym for an electronic mailing list—even if the list is indeed managed by *LISTSERV* software. Wrong: *a LISTSERV list for pet fanciers.* (n.) As *LISTSERV* is a trademark, do not use it as a noun to refer to the electronic mailing list itself or in a generic sense to refer to any e-mail list based on another mailing list management software. The correct way to refer to such a list—whether it is based on *LISTSERV* software or not—is *e-mail list* or *e-discussion list.*

localization (n.) One of the major topics in software and Web development today is *localization*—customizing a software application or a Web site's content and features for a "local" audience. *Localization* goes beyond straight translation to include accommodation for local culture and beliefs. For example, when localizing Web graphics, a non-US citizen may not understand the relationship between an image of a woman office manager faced with a pile of boxes and your company's global shipping services. (v.) *To localize, localized, localizing.* (adj.) *Localization industry.* Also called *internationalization.*

log on, log off (v.), **logon** (adj.), **login, logon** (n.) To *log on* to a network means to connect with the network by submitting the proper user name and/or password to gain access. *Log in* is an alternative for *log on*. To disconnect from the network, one *logs off* or *logs out*. Microsoft recommends against using *log in*; however, in common use, both *log on* and *log in* are acceptable. The *Wired Style Guide* offers the advice that "*log in* and *log out* are more common in the Unix world." We advise using the terms consistently: Pair *log on* with *log off*, and don't switch randomly among the variants in a publication or on a Web site. Use *log on to*, not *log onto*: *The user logged on to the network.* Usage note: It's important to remember that the *logon process* involves authorization. Don't use it for an open access system—don't say *Log on to our Web page*. (adj.) *Logon* can be used as an adjective: *logon password, logon routine.* (n.)

Login. The account name a person uses to connect to a network, Web service, bulletin board service, and so on: *My login name is jsmith.* Also called *logon.*

media (n.) 1. *Media* is technically a plural term (a count noun), with *medium* as its singular. *Media* as a singular term was once understood to refer only to newspapers. But *media* is now widely used as a collective noun to mean all forms of information dissemination, including newspapers, magazines, television, radio, and the Web. That's what *mass media* means, and *media* has become shorthand for that collective (singular) sense. We recommend using the singular in this sentence: *Is the soundbite-hungry media to blame for the negative tenor of political dialog?* 2. *Media* are objects that hold computer data for purposes of backup or distribution. This category of *media* includes diskettes (floppy disks), CD-ROMs, hard disks, and magnetic tapes. 3. In a new-media context, *media* refers to the specific electronic techniques used to present content and can include text, audio, video, graphic enhancement, and animation. The term *mixed media* incorporates several different forms of media. 4. In a computer network, *transmission media* link individual workstations together. Types of *transmission media* include coaxial cable, twisted-pair wire, and fiber-optic cable. (adj.) *Media feeding frenzy.*

meta tag (n.) *Meta tags* are words that describe the content of a Web page so that it can be indexed by a search engine. A casual visitor viewing a page with a Web browser does not see the *meta tags.* While most words with the *meta-*prefix are closed compounds, *meta tag* is preferred as an open compound for clarity by a preponderance of sources.

meta- words The prefix *meta-* means "about" and is usually written as a closed compound with the word it modifies. A *metalanguage* is a language used to describe other languages. A *metafile* is a file that contains other files. The fact that *The Metadata Company* is a registered trademark does not govern the style of the common noun *metadata,* meaning "data about data." The closed form is more frequently used, though *meta-data* is also seen.

mouseover *Jargon.* Closed compound. (n.) The JavaScript technique that allows a Web page element (usually a graphic) to change as the mouse passes over it. (adj.) *Mouseover effects.* Also spelled *mouse-over.* Sometimes called a *rollover.*

multi- words The prefix *multi-* usually adds a connotation of "many," "more than one," or "many times over." Some would hyphenate between the prefix and a root word with an adjacent vowel: *multi-user* vs. *multiuser,* but words beginning with the prefix multi- are usually closed compounds: *multicast,* *multidimensional, multifrequency, multilaunch, multilayer, multilevel, multilingual, multimedia, multimode, multiplexing, multipoint, multiported, multitasking, multithreading, multivendor.*

multimedia (n.) *Multimedia,* used rather loosely to mean "a category of content," "a format," "a means of publication," or all three, includes text, graphics, audio, and video. (adj.) *Multimedia computer, multimedia software. Multimedia software* enables us to create online presentations that incorporate video clips, sound, and animation. See also media.

newsgroup (n.) A *newsgroup* is an online discussion group that is distributed through Usenet, using the Internet protocol Network News Transfer Protocol (NNTP). The Internet is host to thousands of newsgroups. Only online discussion groups that are a part of Usenet are considered newsgroups. Non-Usenet online forums have other names, like *chat rooms* or *Web-based discussions.*

offline (adv.) Disconnected and/or unable to receive data: *The printer is offline. Offline* has taken on the informal connotation of being away from one's computers and the Internet and unreachable by e-mail: *I will be offline while I am on vacation in the Amazon.* (adj.) *Jargon. Offline* can mean non-computerized or not Net-connected—*the offline world* as opposed to *the online world.*

on the fly (adv.) Dynamic Web pages are composed of components collected and served on demand, or *on the fly.* (adj.) Hyphenate the adjective: "*On-the-fly editing* of video is editing live or without stopping the tapes" (Medialink Broadcasting Glossary).

online (adv., adj.) *Online* has many meanings. We recommend using *online* as a closed compound for all of them. *Online* as an adverb can mean "in a computerized format" (versus print): *The tax forms are available both in print and online. Online* may mean "on the Web" or in any digital format. If you're using *online* to mean "digital," be specific, because it has begun to imply the *Web* as a default: *do online research, go online to verify the facts. Online* also refers to electronic equipment being connected and ready to receive data: the printer is *online.* The opposite is offline.

online community (n.) Either the entire population of Web users or a specific niche community formed around a specific portal, Web site, chat room, e-mail list, newsgroup, or blog.

outsource Closed compound. (v.) To use services or resources provided by a consultant or supplier outside a firm.

pageview (n.) A pageview is a Web advertising term that refers to a Web site visitor viewing a page. If a visitor clicks on 12 pages on a Web site, this constitutes 12 *pageviews.* Online advertising rates are often based on the *pageview statistic.*

PDF *Portable Document Format.* (n.) A *PDF* is the type of file created by Adobe's Acrobat software. Also an adjective and a verb: *We PDF'd the file to you yesterday.*

Photoshop (adj.) Adobe *Photoshop* software is used for image editing. Adobe prefers that its trademarks be used as adjectives followed by a generic term (such as *software*). Correct: *Color-correct these images using Photoshop software.* Incorrect: *We need to photoshop these images.* But we all use this word informally as a generic verb.

portal (n.) A *portal* is a Web site that offers a jumping-off point to the Web. *Portals* offer concentrated resources, news, and services to attract and hold repeat visitors. They often offer personalization features that allow registered users to customize the data that the portal will push at sign-in. A *vertical portal* concentrates on a tightly focused niche market, such as engineers or desktop publishers. A *vertical portal* for mechanical engineers is iCrank.com; it offers features such as engineering reference data, links to vendors, software and hardware, technical discussion forums, and news of upcoming conferences. A *horizontal portal* offers a broad range of services and features to appeal to the broadest possible range of people. Major *horizontal portals* such as Excite and Yahoo! offer myriad features, including personalization, free e-mail, a search engine, news, weather, chat rooms, stock quotes, shopping, and horoscopes. Acceptable references are *portal* and *Web portal.* Do not use *portal site.*

preflight *Jargon.* (adj.) Always a closed compound. The thorough review of an electronic publication before it is sent to the printer for output: *preflight check.* (v.) *to preflight. Preflight the annual report files before they go to the printer.*

print-on-demand (**POD**) (n.) *Print-on-demand* is a relatively new process for printing books efficiently and cost-effectively one copy at a time. (adj.) Barnes & Noble signed an agreement with IBM to provide *print-on-demand equipment* for its distribution centers.

pull (adj., v.) The common form of information access across the Web or a computer network, *pull technology* delivers information or data only when a user directly requests it. Clicking on a hyperlink or requesting a file is one way a user *pulls* information from a server. Contrast with *push technology.* See also push.

pure play (adj.) A *pure play* company has its entire operation online. A *pure play* Internet company does not have a bricks-and-mortar presence. Also called a *pure Internet company.*

push (adj.) *Push technology* delivers a program of news and information to a person's computer or handheld device. (v.) Information is delivered or *pushed* to the user either on a preset schedule or upon request. The user specifies what information he or she wants delivered (stock quotes, news headlines, local weather, entertainment news, etc.) and how often. Web portals often feature personal home pages that *push* custom programs of news and information to users who sign up for the service. Contrast with pull technology.

radio button (n.) Two words. *Radio buttons* are used on Web pages and online forms when the person filling out the form must choose one of several options. Like a predigital car radio that had big buttons to push to select a station, *radio buttons* can be selected only one at a time.

real time, real-time (n., adj.) Something that is telecast, broadcast, or relayed when it is actually happening, as opposed to a recorded or delayed transmission event. *Millions of viewers tuned into the concert broadcast over the Internet in real time.* (adj.) Hyphenated. *Real-time animation, real-time clock, real-time compression, real-time conferencing, real-time image, real-time operating system, real-time video, real-time information system.*

repurpose (v.) To plan for the reuse of content and/or electronic coding, graphics, and layout for multiple applications, such as using the same content for a newsletter that is printed and e-mailed, posted on a Web page, and sent as a podcast. Such strategic positioning of content early in the publishing process allows it to be distributed to reach audiences in their preferred format and medium.

resolution—high-resolution, low-resolution (n., adj.) In graphic arts and computing, *resolution* refers to the fineness of detail and clarity of an image. The term is used with bitmapped graphic images, printers, scanners, and monitors. The more dots or pixels per square inch, the higher the *resolution* and quality. *Low-resolution* and *high-resolution* are most often used as hyphenated adjectives: *a high-resolution image, a low-resolution image. Jargon: high-res* or *hi-res, low-res.*

scalable (adv.) Business jargon adapted from the computing world—means capable of being expanded or reduced to the necessary and cost-effective size and scope. *This software is fully scalable; it can serve anyone from home-based Web creators to design teams at major corporate sites.* (v.) *to scale up* and *to scale down* (preferred to *upsize* and *downsize*).

secure (adj.) A secure Web server conforms to one of the major security protocols to prevent unauthorized or destructive access. When a server or an area of a Web site is *not* secure, refer to it as *nonsecure* (not *insecure*).

setup, set up, Setup (n.) The way a computer's hardware and software is configured is its *setup* (one word). *Setup* (initial cap) refers to the installation program that comes with most applications (setup.exe): *Run Setup to install the program on your computer.* (adj.) The adjective is spelled as one word: *setup routine.* (v.) *Set up* is two words when used as a verb meaning to install or configure hardware or software.

sign on (v.) *Sign on* is used as a synonym for log on when referring to connecting to a network. *Log on* is the preferred term. (adj.) *sign-on name.*

spec (n.) As a noun, *spec(s)* is short for *specification(s)*, as in *The specs for that print job are 20 copies, in Garamond type and doublespaced.* (v.) As a verb, *to spec* is short for *specify* and means "to write instructions for." Spelling of *spec* as a verb includes *speccing* and *specced* or *spec'd.* Because it's an informal word to begin with, we prefer the informal conjugations: *spec'ing* and *spec'd. Specked* is not preferable, implying as it does the footprints of flies. *Working to spec* means "doing it just as planned."

startup (n., adj.) Much like *voicemail*, which began life in the first edition of this glossary as *voice mail* but by summer of 2000 moved to the solid form that is now in widest use. *Startup* began life in newspapers like the *Washington Post* as *start-up* and is now most often seen closed up. A *startup* is a new company, often a new Internet company. (v.) Use as two words: *To start up yet another online bookstore would be madness until Amazon figures it out.*

techno- words Closed compounds: *technoanxiety, technobabble, technocrat, technofiend, technographer, technologitis, technophobe, technophile, technostress.*

tele- words Words beginning with the prefix *tele-* are proliferating. They are always written as closed compounds. Some of the recent occurrences of *tele-* we have found: *telecommute, teleconference, telecommuting agreement, teleworker, telework, telework coordinator, telework agreement, telework inventory, telework program.*

upload (v.) To transmit a file from your computer to a remote location such as an FTP site. See also download.

URLs (n.) Some companies and organizations style their Web address so people can remember their name: HowThingsWork.com. But because most browsers automatically add the *http://* and *www.* elements to a URL, the contemporary style is to leave them off when giving a URL in text. Thus, to refer you to the companion Web site for this book, we need to write only **eeicom.com/press/istyle**. When the URL is for a secure site that begins with https:// or a site that uses a protocol other than HTTP (such as an FTP site), those cues are necessary.

video- words Words formed with the *video* prefix are usually, but not always, closed compounds: *videocam* (but *video camera*), *videoconference*, *videodisc*, *videogame*, *videotape* (but *video adapter* and *video port*).

viral marketing (n.) A marketing technique in which people are encouraged to contact friends to recommend the product.

virtual terms (adj.) Virtual is added to just about any word to add the sense of not real, as in existing in conceptual space but not physical space. Terms including *virtual* are written as open compounds: *virtual office*, *virtual employees*, *virtual meeting*, *virtual reality*, *virtual desktop*, *virtual private network*, *virtual disk*.

voicemail (n.) *Voicemail* is used to refer to both the system ("All the employees have voicemail") and, more informally, to the individual messages ("I left you several voicemails"). This term is a closed compound in most sources researched. (adj.) *Voicemail system, voicemail message.*

-ware words (n.) *-ware* words are a takeoff on hardware/software and generally refer to classes of software products, such as *groupware*, *intraware*, and *middleware*. They usually appear as closed compounds, like their predecessor words. For example: *shareware, freeware, shovelware, vaporware, firmware, wetware, bioware.*

Web page (n., adj.) It's hard to say exactly what a *Web page* is—the term is used loosely—but nontech people loosely understand what it means. A *home page* is not necessarily the opening page of a site; a so-called *Web page* can be many pages long (in terms of both screenfuls and sections), but it's not necessarily the same as a *Web site* (though, literally and practically speaking, a site is a collection of electronic pages formatted in HTML). Is that perfectly clear? Two universities define the term this way for their site users (punctuation theirs):

> A **web page** provides access to networked information and databases via a part of the Internet called the World Wide Web. The University of Delaware Library has a web "site" called a **home page**. The Library home page provides access to Library information, services and databases, including the Library Networked Databases. The Library Networked Databases page provides access to Library databases that are networked on the Internet. This way, you can access several Library databases from a single web page...

> **Web page**—entry point in a World Wide Web information site; often called a home page. To create your own Web page, see *Your Auburn University Web Page*.

The whole schmear, soup to nuts, is a *Web site*. Some people take the shortcut of using *Web page* to mean "any or all of the content on a site" and as a synonym for *Web site* as well. It would be clearer to use *Web page* to refer to a single document (corresponding to one specific URL) in a collection of content at a site. Don't hold your breath, though.

Web words (n.) *Web* is capitalized when it stands alone, short for the proper noun *World Wide Web*. (adj.) *Web* is also capitalized when it forms part of an open compound, as in *Web technology*, *Web address*, *Web-based* ("Web-based merchants"), *Web-centric* ("a Web-centric commerce model"), *Web browser*, *Web page*, *Web portal*, *Web ring*, *Web site*. There are a few cases in which *Web* forms part of a closed compound; in these cases it is lowercased: *webmaster*, *webzine*, *webcast*, *webonomics*.

webcast (n.) One word, lowercased—patterned on the word it is based on, *broadcast*. A *webcast* is a transmission of an event like a concert or conference over the Internet. The event may be live or recorded. Interestingly, this is almost always used as a noun and shows no urgent trend toward being verbed.

Web-enabled (adj.) An application or enterprise that makes use of the Web but is not completely based on the Web.

webmaster (n.) *Webmaster* was originally a take-off on *postmaster*. Like *postmaster*, *webmaster* is written as a closed compound, and Web is not capitalized. The *webmaster* is the person responsible for building and maintaining a Web site.

workaround (n.) A *workaround* is the creative solution we develop when an existing system either doesn't work properly or doesn't cover all the contingencies. Like, you know, when we're not sure whether *countywide* and *statewide* are correct just because *worldwide* is. Why is it *never-ending* but *everlasting* and *nevermore?* The creative solution we come up with is often "what feels least wrong."

workflow Closed compound. (n.) *Workflow* is an organizational concept, like workgroup. A *workgroup* is task-centric. In an organizational setting, *workflow* consists of specific processes that need to be accomplished and who needs to do them in order to attain a specified outcome.

workstation (n.) A *workstation,* when referring to a computer, usually means a high-powered database and graphics-crunching personal computer. In a network context, workstation refers to an individual's personal computer—a network client as opposed to the server.

zine *Jargon.* (n.) A *zine* is an informal newsletter/magazine. It usually appeals to a tightly defined niche and has slightly underground appeal. When a *zine* goes online, it becomes a webzine or e-zine. These digital zines have the same offbeat niche appeal, but they reside on Web sites or are distributed by e-mail newsletter. We spell *webzine* as a closed compound with a lowercase *w.*

19 TERMS THAT LEAVE AN I-FLAVOR ON THE BEDPOST OVERNIGHT

NetLingo, Erin Jansen's Web site, claims it has thousands of definitions that easily explain the Internet and the online world of business, technology, and communication for new users, industry professionals, students, and educators. We'd add that the terms listed can be eye-opening for editors who don't want to be clueless about Netglish. Jansen has kindly allowed us to present what she believes are the top 19 tech terms of 2006 that have become common expressions. (On netlingo.com, many terms in the definitions are cross-linked to further definitions—one way Web text is superior to the printed page.)

1. bandwidth. The technical definition involves the difference between two frequencies and the amount of information that can flow through a channel as expressed in cycles per second (hertz). It also refers to the range of frequencies (not the speed) or the measured amount of information that can be transmitted over a connection: The higher the frequency, the higher the bandwidth and the greater the capacity of a channel to carry information. For a digital channel, bandwidth is defined in bits per second (bps). For an analog channel, it depends on the type and method of modulation used to encode the data.

Broadcast *TV channels*, for example, all have the same bandwidth, by FCC rule. You may hear *bandwidth* described as the amount of time it takes a *Web page* to fully load (although this is incorrect) or as the amount of traffic on a *Web site* (this is also incorrect, but widely used). Internet users refer to larger graphics as "bandwidth hogs," because they take up so much room and download so slowly. Another slang use describes the inability to think about or do multiple things at once, as in "I don't have the bandwidth to deal with your request right now." If a person is described as having "low bandwidth," it means he or she is considered slow on the uptake.

2. plug-and-play. A standard for add-in hardware that requires it to identify itself on demand. Most computer systems are designed to be plug-and-play: You can buy it, bring it home, plug it in, and start playing. This makes it easier for people who consider themselves computer illiterate to use a computer, because they don't need to install devices or configure drivers—it does most of the work for you. There's also something known as "plug-and-print," a behind-the-screens technology that improves the way printers and computers communicate. Slang usage refers to a new employee who doesn't need training. For example, "The new girl is...totally plug-and-play."

3. opt-out/downtime. When a user asks to be removed from any kind of *online program*. For example, if you no longer want to receive an e-mail newsletter, you can opt out. Note that there is a difference between opting out and unsubscribing. You may only unsubscribe to something you have previously subscribed to, but you may opt out of something you have never joined in the first place. For example, if you fill out an online form to register or sign up for something, you may see a "yes" automatically checked in a radio button to indicate that you wish to receive something. Unless you manually uncheck the yes, you will be added to some kind of marketing list. Opt-out also refers to a type of service that assumes inclusion unless informed otherwise.

4. radar screen. The range of interests that a company or person is focused on. For example, "With voice portals on everyone's radar screen, a wide variety of companies are now trying to figure out how they can voice-enable their businesses." Another example: "There is no *technology* that allows him to use a Palm Pilot; in fact, the blind are not on anybody's radar screen yet."

5. acronyms: FYI, SNAFU, TMI. [This entry links to a NetLingo List of Acronyms & Text Messaging Shorthand—many of them humorous and slightly profane.] Commonly seen wherever people get online—including instant messaging, cell phones, PDAs, Web sites, newsgroup postings, and blogs. Acronyms have always been an integral part of computer culture, and they have spawned a new language on the Internet. Online enthusiasts, primarily millennials, are learning that shorthand is called "acronyms," but this is incorrect. The difference between acronyms and shorthand is that with acronyms, you pronounce the letters of the abbreviation as a new word (for example, FUBAR is pronounced "foo-bar"). In contrast, the letters of shorthand terms are pronounced one-by-one and not pronounced as a word (for example, FYI is pronounced "F-Y-I"). The difference between shorthand and initialisms (another type of abbreviation) is that the latter refers to the shortening of a word itself, for example "esp" for "especially." The online practice is to refer to any shorthand or abbreviation as an acronym. The majority of the expressions you see are not acronyms but rather shorthand used while text messaging or IM'ing. BTW: If you ever see someone TYPING AN ENTIRE SENTENCE IN ALL CAPITAL LETTERS that means SHOUTING! It is not proper netiquette to TYPE IN ALL CAPS (even in e-mail); in fact, it's annoying. People with limited eyesight may use all caps to see the words better; otherwise, TURN THE CAPS LOCK OFF, unless you're using an acronym or shorthand. [Ed. Note: What Jansen calls *shorthand* we would call *initialism* and what she calls *initialism* is actually more like *shorthand*—no wonder millennials are confused, if editors are, too.]

6. 86'd. It means "out of" or "over" or "to get rid of." This expression comes from the restaurant industry, where it's the code on the computers to signify that the restaurant has run out of a particular dish. It is an acronym or text message used in online chat, IM, e-mail, blogs, or newsgroup postings. [Commonly heard at bars, i.e., people not being served anymore because they're drunk.]

7. multitasking. [Listed but not defined on NetLingo; definition here from Wikipedia.] Multitasking may refer to any of the following:

1. Computer multitasking—the apparent simultaneous performance of two or more tasks by a computer's central processing unit.
2. Derived from the first sense, multitasking is the colloquial term for a human being's simultaneous handling of multiple tasks.
3. Media multitasking could refer to using a computer, mp3, or any other media in conjunction with another medium.
4. "Polychronistic time" is business jargon for multitasking.

8. users/visitors. The term defines the online audience; it also refers to anyone who uses a computer. It comes from techies, who refer to people as "***computer users.***" The word "users" is not yet in the **American Heritage** *Dictionary*, but "user-friendly" made it. In the past, "user" meant drug user...does this say something about how we're all getting addicted to the online world? Let's relish the fact that we're the first group of people ever to be "online users!"

9. interface. In a general sense, the interface is the part of a program that interacts between a user and an application, meaning it is what you see on the computer screen. The word usually means "user interface," which consists of a set of operating system commands, graphical display formats, and other features designed for use on a computer or a program. A "graphical user interface" (GUI; pronounced goo-ey) provides users with a picture-oriented, user-friendly way to see what is on a computer system. A "programming interface" consists of the set of statements, functions, options, and other ways of expressing program instructions and data. The interface is also a special point of entry into the software or operating system, where programmers can work on the underlying code. Another definition of interface is the connection between two applications or two hardware devices that facilitates the exchange of data. "To interface" is to make an appropriate physical connection between two pieces of hardware so the equipment can communicate or work together effectively. The word has permeated into mainstream culture; "to interface" means to communicate with another person or object.

10. rant and rave. To go on and on about something you feel passionate about. Users often rant and rave about topics in newsgroups. "Rant" implies negative feelings; "rave" implies admiration.

11. Film @11. Reference to TV commercials for the late local news; a sarcastic phrase used in newsgroups or chat rooms in reaction to an overwrought argument. For example, "Imminent death of the Net predicted. Film at 11." The phrase has also become a funny kind of "copout" at the end of a news article or explanation, as if to say, "It's too early to draw any conclusions that you'll hold me to later." For example, if the author isn't sure where a particular ***technology*** is headed, he or she is signifying that the debate will continue to rage on. For example, "A hot topic is the future of ***e-commerce*** and the B2B sector. Film at 11." Simply, it means there's more to come.

12. cybersquatting. The practice of purchasing a ***domain name*** that contains a well-known ***trademark*** or commercial name (for example, generalelectric.com). The intent is not to develop it into a Web site but rather to sell it to the rightful owner for a big profit. This practice is being contested in various legal battles; usually, the company, not the cybersquatter, wins.

13. navigate. The act of moving around the Web by clicking on hypertext links (or paths) that take you from one Web page to another. As you navigate, you move from one computer to another and from one server to another without realizing it.

14. McLuhanisms: *medium is the message, global village, digital revolution.* A term for a catchy phrase or slogan coined by **Marshall McLuhan**, popular writer and intellectual thinker during the digital revolution. For example, he said, "The medium is the message," meaning that the form of media has a greater impact on society than the content.

15. Google (Google, Inc.). A company founded in 1998 by Larry Page and Sergey Brin, two Stanford Ph.D. candidates who developed a technologically advanced method for finding information on the Internet. Its most famous product is a hybrid search engine that ranks the popularity of results that match your keyword search. It has an index of billions of Web pages. Google focuses primarily on delivering the best search experience on the Web by providing a search site and licensing its search technology to commercial sites. Web sites are permitted to freely use Google technology—such as Google Local and Google Maps—on their own sites. Like many great Internet terms, Google has morphed into a general term for "search," as in "Did you Google your date to find out more about him?"

Using Google's name as a verb may impinge on trademark. The company makes the distinction between using the word "Google" to describe using Google to search the Internet, and using the word to describe searching the Internet. [Ed. Note: Good luck with enforcing that distinction, Google!] The company has entered various industries, such as telecommunications, and the Google Web site has expanded to offer many extra features. For example, Deja News (now known as "Google Groups" following its acquisition by Google) is a database front-end for searching the Usenet newsgroups, which form the largest information utility in existence. Known simply as the search engine for the newsgroups, it provides users with complete access to Usenet data since 1995. Google Groups offers the complete 20-year Usenet Archive, with over 700 million messages. Google has become so popular that a Swedish couple named their baby boy Oliver Google Kai.

16. 404. An acronym or text message used in online chat, IM, e-mail, blogs, or newsgroup postings. It means *"I haven't got a clue."*

17. DBEYR. An acronym used in online chat, IM, e-mail, blogs, or newsgroup postings. It means "Don't believe everything you read."

18. morph. [Listed without definition on NetLingo; definition from Wikipedia.] Morphing is a special effect in motion pictures and animations that changes one image into another through a seamless transition. Most often it is used to show one person turning into another through some magical or technological means or as part of a fantasy or surreal sequence. Traditionally, such a depiction was achieved through cross-fading techniques on film. Since the early 1990s, these techniques have been replaced by computer software that creates more realistic transitions.

19. just-in-time (JIT). Originally, this phrase described a compiler that turns Java bytecode, for example, into instructions that can be sent directly to a *processor*. Now it usually refers to a system of inventory control, supplier relationships, quality control, and so on. Slang usage has morphed the meaning into something that can be handled or assimilated quickly, such as just-in-time training: small, easily digestible pieces of information.

11

Coda: The Future of the Book

Books have not changed much structurally since the Egyptians started using papyrus scrolls around 2400 BC. Gutenberg made more books available to more people, but the technology of the book stayed the same until recently. Now we're seeing alternative ways to create, use, distribute, and market books.

Electronic books are the wave of the present, though not all publishers are on board—and the hype hasn't allayed reservations based on, frankly, the disappointing state of the art of the e-reading experience.

But audio books and electronic books expand the ways the content of books can be accessed. CD-ROMs packed as supplements to reference works and software manuals tremendously enhance the usefulness of the printed word. And with widespread commitment to sustainable publishing practices—not to mention the rising costs of paper, ink, print production, and storage of inventory—the business case for e-books, especially titles printed only as needed, is impressive.

However, an awful lot of human beings have an irrational, deeply held love of the printed book, perhaps hard-wired into some of us via the recessive papyrus gene. Still, this is a book about the future.

MASS DIGITIZATION OF BOOKS

Google Inc. and Microsoft Corp. are leading the way in digitizing massive numbers of books, and more texts can be read online than ever before. The quality of the scanned image continues to improve, though critics remain unimpressed by the state of e-readers.

The Internet allows almost anyone to enjoy free access to books through public libraries, and growing numbers of library patrons are seizing the opportunity to access books online. As the *New York Times* reported, "The newest books in the New York Public Library don't take up any shelf space. They are electronic books—3,000 titles' worth—and the library's 1.8 million card-holders can point and click through the collection" ("Libraries Reach Out, Online," Dec. 4, 2004, nytimes.com/2004/12/09/technology/circuits/09libr.html?ex=1260248400&en=bc31f3ce53fcf024&ei=5090&partner=rssuserland).

Many library e-books are free, while others can be used for a nominal fee. The European Library is an example of a portal into books and magazine and journal articles, enabling scholars to access materials for research.

Online documents can enhance other components of a digital collection. For example, at the Paul Laurence Dunbar Digital Collection, a visitor can browse the author's books, read his poetry, hear his poems read aloud, and view photos of the poet. Technology allows various resources to be compiled into a collection and accessed by visitors (libraries.wright.edu/special/dunbar).

Google Book Search works with partners, including libraries, to make it easier for people to find the books they want. Books beyond copyright coverage are available full-text; for those still covered by copyright, relevant information and excerpts are available to help readers make decisions about buying them. Google Book Search enables readers to view and download a book or to find out where they can buy it or borrow it.

But some US publishers have taken would-be content aggregators to court to stop them from unauthorized digitizing of copyrighted books, whether for free distribution or resale. Litigation by individual publishers to keep copyrighted works out of third-party databases will likely continue, while Google and others maintain that they're performing a valuable public service.

With regard to sales, publishing giants Random House and HarperCollins, have "taken a step into cyberspace" by allowing customers to browse their books online, as reported by CNN.com early in 2007 ("Publishers OK Online Book Browsing," Feb. 28, 2007, cnn.com/2007/TECH/internet/02/28/book.browsing.reut/index.html).

And Amazon.com has revolutionized book shopping online by enabling shoppers to preview the table of contents and selected pages of a book to help them decide what to buy—while safeguarding content from being printed out or downloaded.

So for some titles, a customer has the choice of reading an e-book free online in a library, checking out a print or electronic copy for a limited time, or buying it as e-book from an e-bookstore; previewing its table of contents and an excerpt on a bookselling site and buying a printed copy online for delivery; or using the Web to check on reviewer comments, the TOC, price, and availability, then driving to a local bricks-and-mortar bookstore to buy a printed copy. For now, it seems, the Web supports the business of selling printed books more successfully than e-books.

E-BOOKS AND USABILITY

Reading a book in the comfort of home. Carrying it to the airport, a soccer practice field, or your doctor's office waiting room. Lending it to a friend. Those are illustrations of the three advantages of 3-D books: They can be savored incrementally at will; they're portable; and they can be shared with as many others as we like.

Electronic book-reader vendors are trying to incorporate features that allow people to read them almost as comfortably as they read physical books; for example, people who like to write in paper books and tab pages can now do the equivalent in e-books. If you haven't tried reading an electronic book, visit Open Library at openlibrary.org. The experience of reading the full text of an online book, complete with scrolling pages, illustrations, and sound, is truly interactive (which is exactly what some people dislike—they want to lose themselves in a book, not interact with it).

Specialized e-book technology is also being developed to facilitate reading for those who cannot: the blind. The number of audible books is very limited, but text-to-speech software makes any e-book accessible to anyone who can hear. You can already listen to a book on an iPod or read it on a cell phone handheld screen, Sony has a new reader with a special black and white computer screen that replicates the look of ink on paper, although this device is expensive and aimed at early adopters.

Jane Litte, a blogger who writes about the perils and joys of the e-reading experience, offers "unsolicited tips on how to make publishing better for the human reader" along with reviews of e-books and e-bookstores. Her open letter on her site—dearauthor.com (stamped Feb. 18, 2007, and reprinted here with permission)—blasts one new e- reader.

This blog entry shows (1) the power of passionately documented criticism from knowledgeable commentators (bloggers are a threat to what's known as online "reputation management"); (2) the tart humor, punchy language, and distrust of corporate agendas often seen in blogging; and (3) the high expectations of the human readers entirely willing to adopt new publishing technologies—but too savvy not to call a dud a dud. Underlined words are links to related information, which provide context for the uninitiated without interrupting the train of thought:

Adobe Labs Cooks Up Worst Ebook Reader in Ebook Reader History

Dear Adobe,

I have often derided the Adobe Acrobat format for ebooks. I have told people on this blog, in emails, on message boards, that this is my least favorite format and that you should only buy this format when there is NO

OTHER OPTION. Buying an Adobe ebook, particularly one that requires authentication to read it, is akin to <u>shaving your head</u> when you are one of the most recognizable people in the world and, at one time, were one of the most beautiful people in the world.

You've come out with a great new software called <u>Adobe Digital Editions</u>, for those people who love ebooks. And by great, I mean, if the reader was an island and had no choice but to choose Adobe's software or be eaten by cannibals. You seem to think that readers want Adobe to control the reading experience because we readers can't possibly know what we want.

Adobe Digital Editions only has four font sizes. You can't type in the percentage you want, it has a small *a* and a large *a* and that controls the font size for the book. Adobe assumes it knows exactly what four font sizes you want. It also assumes when you will want two pages per screen or one page per screen. You don't get to choose.

You also believe that readers won't mind that when they use the "page up/page down" keys or the arrow keys entire sections are skipped. And you, paternally, like to believe that readers will WANT to always upgrade to the new and supposedly better version. Because everyone is moving to Vista and everyone has downloaded and installed IE 7, right? Too bad, so sad, for the users of Adobe Digital Editions because it will REQUIRE the reader to download the upgrade before she can read those ebooks she paid for.

Worse yet, is that this reading program is not exactly free. What do I mean by that. Well, in the licensing portion of the FAQ at Adobe's site, it tells us that the following:

> To offset Adobe's costs in developing and operating Digital Editions and its associated content protection infrastructure, Adobe will provide dynamic context-based ads in the user interface of the Digital Editions application. We hope to make these ads tasteful, minimally distracting, and useful. A premium version of Digital Editions will be available on a subscription basis (price TBD), and content publishers using Adobe DRM technology will have the option to disable contextual ads. NOTE: Ads are not enabled in the initial beta releases.

So, I pay for the book and in order for me to read the book, I still get my special content-related ads unless I pay for a premium version or the content publisher disables the ads? No wait, they'll be tasteful and only "minimally" distracting. I can just imagine the increased uptick in name dropping in books as we get Adobe's version of Google Ad Words. And what about those Avon Red or Harlequin Spice books. What "tasteful" ads are going to be generated with those stories?

Go you for creating a reading environment that is actually worse than the one you had before. I love it when big companies regress. Thanks, but I'll sit this program out. It makes more sense to shave my hair off. At least I would be in control of that situation.

Best regards,
Jane

The way bloggers create a sense of community is by allowing others to respond to their postings—thus opening the discussion to consensus, disagreement, and new information. One of Litte's readers replied sourly:

Not only did I have to download several versions of Reader 8, and then when this wouldn't work, 7, which ALSO would not work, with their huge and slow installers, I was then prompted to download the beta version of Digital Editions, which was annoying enough in itself: the damn book would not download within Digital Editions. If I tried to open the book without Editions open first, I got a weird error which told me nothing useful. If I tried when it was open I could see the cover of the book...but that was all. I could find nothing on the website to explain any of this, or to report bugs, which this obviously was. Version 7 didn't work either, for some more strange errors, despite a fresh install. What did work? Using the existing Version 6 (Pro) on a work PC. Unfortunately version 6 is not downloadable anymore.

Getting trapped in fatal-error loops between software editions isn't anyone's idea of a party. That's just one of the reasons the book you're holding in your hand right now isn't an e-book. The next person who asks us, "Shouldn't a book about Internet style be a digital book?" is going to get sent to Litte's office.

Ease of access and cost-efficient production will be defined relatively, conditionally, and personally by different publishers and consumers—and the models and ground rules will change over time. The capability for user customization of the reading experience for maximum comfort is, however, a universal expectation—and one still largely unmet.

THE COST OF CHANGE

Technology is not the only determinant in how books will change—three other factors will determine how they will be used and ultimately valued in the future: cost, convenience, and personal preference.

Cost is the number one determinant of how and whether people obtain books, which have historically been fairly expensive. Technology has lowered publishing costs and enabled Internet users to access free or extremely low-cost books, including used copies. Opportunities abound for finding out-of-print and hard-to-find books (though at a premium). Whether electronically or in print, more books are more available than ever before; in fact, it's estimated that about 3,000 new books are published every day.

The full text of some books can be found online at no charge. Many of these works are not part of mainstream publishing—specialized audiences now have enormously increased opportunities to visit collections of narrow interest. The Internet makes it easy to read works that are not available in print and books one is not inclined to physically acquire. Search technology motivates many students and researchers to choose e-books.

College textbooks are a special case. Some students facing the rising cost of textbooks have turned to e-books. But despite campaigns to make textbooks free online, the number of students using e-books has not risen dramatically. An April 2006 *New York Times* article reported that students preferred e-books "typically 40 percent less than a new textbook and 20 percent less than a used one" ("The Bottom Line on E-Textbooks," by Edward Wyatt, April 23, 2006, nytimes.com/2006/04/23/education/edlife/innovate .html?ex=1172811600&en=d68b2341189033b6&ei=5070).

Low price and the ease of downloading an e-book are of only so much value to those students. After all, an overdue library e-book can instantly lock a user out, regardless of that midterm exam tomorrow morning. And sometimes students simply want to own and keep the physical book—or resell it.

STORING BOOKS

Space is a consideration for readers, whether they're students, librarians, or just lifelong book lovers. Accessing books electronically requires no shelf space. Storage is also no problem for downloaded texts: About 14,000 average-sized books will fit on a $2 double-layer DVD, and many times that will fit on the newer blue-laser DVDs. The next generation of removable memory—holographic DVDs that use two lasers—will be able to store the text (although not the images) of the entire Library of Congress (130 million items) on six disks ("What is HDVD," Tech-FAQ, tech-faq.com/hvd.shtml). Ultimately, the entire Library of Congress will fit in a space the size of a sugar cube.

Still, it's hard to imagine not having some three-dimensional books to touch and admire on the shelf, and to pull out at random for the pleasure of recalling a few lines or seeing a cherished inscription here and there. Online books and those on a binary physical storage medium cannot give you that tactile quality.

But ordering physical books online has been a cost-saving change for shoppers. Bookstores do not have to stock as deep a backlist, which may be a business-buster for land bookstores but allows bookbuyers to troll for the lowest price and fastest, cheapest delivery method. Some books have become so cheap we can buy them during a layover at the airport and pitch them into the recycling bin at the end of the flight.

Print-on-demand, which lets publishers print books only when an order arrives, is a cost-saving measure for publishers and readers. The dream of in-store kiosks where individuals can print a single copy of a book on the premises hasn't been realized, but pay-per-print is growing in popularity on the Web. Readers pay for the books they want and are granted instant access, either permanently or for a limited time, to save and print them out. At least in theory, when storage and distribution are no longer a concern, more titles can be kept "in print"—or more accurately, printable.

PRESERVING PAST TREASURES

Though it's too late for the Royal Library of Alexandria, electronic preservation has been a treasure-saver for many libraries, museums, and other institutions that conserve books of great cultural value. Such books may be too delicate or valuable for the public to handle. Electronic preservation of documents means that more esoteric collections can be found online. E-books have allowed public access to many collections that would otherwise be seen by only a few, and only by appointment; researchers are delving into books that were once locked away because of their vulnerability. E-books also reduce the opportunity for vandalism or theft of rare books.

CNN.com reported that the Library of Congress received a $2 million grant for a program to digitize thousands of works, with a major focus on "brittle books"—those at most risk of damage, and therefore inaccessible ("Library of Congress to Digitize Brittle Books," cnn.com/2007/TECH/02/01/digital.books.ap/).

E-PUBLISHING IS A CULTURAL SHIFT

Plain and simple, e-books and print-on-demand are revolutionizing publishing. Authors whose work is not deemed profitable by publishing houses can put their text up on a Web site and offer it free or charge for downloads—although that involves an honor system because, once online text is available to one person, it can be transferred to anyone else.

Copyright law can be difficult to enforce online. In 2000, Stephen King famously conducted an experiment in which readers were asked to pay for each installment of a book as he put it online. But so many people simply passed the installments on to friends that he abandoned the project, as reported by *Wired* magazine and others ("Whither 'The Plant,'" M. J. Rose, Nov. 28, 2000, wired.com/news/culture/0,1284,40356,00.html).

If unagented individuals now have an easier route to publishing, collaboration has also reached new heights. Books have been written by multiple authors as Web wikis (essentially, public files that anyone can edit or contribute to) and as plain text on a cell phone, literally phoned in. Amazon.com promotes an e-book service that allows anyone who owns digital rights to a book to make the text available electronically. And companies like Lulu.com specialize in publishing and printing solely from the Web.

A recent *New York Times* online article about LibraryThing, a Web site for bibliophiles that has been around since 2005, nicely shows the convergence of several trends made possible by technology. "Social networking for bookworms," the site has been described by a happy user. The March 4, 2007, article by Anne Eisenberg begins:

> When many people think of online social networking, they picture Web sites where the young and the restless discuss their love lives and their favorite bands. But Kathryn Havemann, 60, of Dayton, Ohio, has joined a different sort of Web-based network—one where people are linked by a more sedate interest: their book collections.

Havemann, described as an indexing analyst at LexisNexis, was pictured alongside a computer with stacks of the books she owns behind her. "I would never put my life out on the Internet," she said, "except through my books."

The idea of the site, which claims 150,000 members, allows book collectors to easily enter a list of what they're reading, or their whole library. A portable barcode scanner can be used to upload as many as 500 entries at a time onto LibraryThing—an inventory that can be kept private or shared with others. The site's founder, Tim Spalding, a former classic scholar and now a Web developer, uses data collected from members to recommend books they may want to read—or skip. Other member benefits include searching the Library of Congress and 70 other world libraries; tagging books with category keywords (WWII, Victorian, philosophy of science, vampires, theology, dogs) that help organize a library while also helping kindred spirits search for and find each other; and sorting books according to personal tags like "books that mention Venice," "books that touch on digital photography," and "books I've loaned out."

The site carries no advertising but is supported by commissions from Amazon.com for books bought through the site, and by member fees. Other sites (for example, Shelfari and aNobii) are also building online book cataloging and social networking services. Havemann summed up her LibraryThing experience: "It's wonderful to know there are many other crazy people out there who are absolutely addicted to books." And they like to talk about books.

At the other end of the spectrum, a press release (March 6, 2007) from IIL Publishing-New York, a division of the International Institute for Learning, crowed: "Publisher enters into the hi-tech arena of searchable and downloadable books." It is singing the song being sung by many other corporate, academic, and STM (scientific, technical, and medical) publishers who want to survive and flourish in the coming decade:

> IIL has been producing quality, out-of-the-box business and project management books since September 2005. In addition to growing a flourishing eBook business, IIL Publishing-New York is now aiming to break ground by participating in new book ventures that use cutting edge technology.
>
> The niche publishing house is taking a leap forward with two new online book venues. IIL Publishing-New York books will now be included in the new Windows Live Book Search (http://publisher.live.com/) and Google Book Search (http://books.google.com/) for FREE browsing access to the public. IIL Publishing-New York books will be available for purchase once readers determine they want them.
>
> "With each book we publish we aim to be ground breaking," said Judith W. Umlas, publisher, IIL Publishing-New York. "Working with Windows Live Book Search and Google Book Search is a natural step in the right direction to give our new publishing division the opportunity to be a part of the innovative online publishing world...."
>
> With their global customers in mind, IIL Publishing-New York wants to make sure its books are easily accessible and quickly consumed by project managers and other busy, time-hungry professionals. The company chose to take part in the exciting venture with Windows Live Book Search and Google Book Search because these ventures, too, are pushing the envelope in book making and customer accessibility and satisfaction.

Out-of-the-box books. Cutting-edge technology. Niche-publishing house. New online book venues. FREE browsing access. The innovative online publishing world. Digitize all of the world's books. Online search service. Powerful user tools. Convenient availability from online bookstores as e-books from e-bookstores. Distribution and marketing partnerships. Global customers. Easily accessible. Quickly consumed. Pushing the envelope in customer satisfaction. Those options and attributes all belong in the toolkit of the book publisher of the near future. Probably. Maybe.

IS ANYBODY READING ALL THESE BOOKS?

Edward Tenner (edwardtenner.com), senior research associate of the Lemelson Center for the History of Invention and Innovation at the National Museum of American History, wrote cogently about the market for books.

In his article, "So Many Books, So Few Readers" (*U.S. 1 Newspaper*, May 12, 2004), Tenner made the point that the printed word has not become "a noble anachronism crushed between televised entertainment and burgeoning electronic information resources, from CD-ROMs and audio books to online hypertext." But all content vies with all other content for attention in a content-glutted world; *aliteracy*, the reluctance of the literate to read any more than they have to, is as powerful a factor as digital technology:

> Paradoxically, it was the rise of computing that propelled the book's enhanced role as prestigiously presented information, and the Web and other digital technology that helped spur book authorship. But this in turn has given publishing and authorship a new set of problems.
>
> One of the surprise critical hits of 2003 was "So Many Books" by the Mexican critic Gabriel Zaid.... Fifty years after the introduction of television, he writes, the number of titles published worldwide each year has increased fourfold from 250,000 to 1 million—from 100 books for every million humans to 167. A book is published somewhere in the world every 30 seconds.
>
> Zaid sees the true problem in the hopeless disproportion between the flood of books and the time and physical space of readers already overwhelmed by the larger information deluge. The speed of publication, Zaid writes, makes us "exponentially more ignorant. If a person reads a book a day, he would be neglecting to read 4,000 others, published the same day."
>
> Books have multiplied partly because they have become less and less important as information storage technologies. As our dependence on them has shrunk, their number and variety has increased, and their status has been if anything enhanced by the attention that the Web has showered on them through online bookselling and discussion groups.
>
> Books have [also] flourished because, despite massive increases in computing power, electronic media often were less efficient than they appeared. The CD-ROM seemed the medium of the future by the early 1990s. But beyond reference publishing and specialized offerings, the CD-ROM let the publishing industry down. Without standardized user interfaces or convenient authoring tools, they were time-consuming both to produce and to use and not readily browsed in retail stores. (When did you last see one in a bookstore, except for those embedded in thick technical tomes?)
>
> It is true that electronic books—those made available as computer files displayed either on portable devices or computer screens—have sunnier

prospects than CD-ROMs. [But] dedicated reading hardware has so far been disappointing. Electronic paper? Philips Research Laboratories of the Netherlands...announced a breakthrough, but no commercial release date has been set. But the real limits to e-books are legal and economic rather than technical....

Most surprisingly, [printed] books survive because technology has made it much easier to write and publish them....

[But] despite the Internet-powered boom in book collecting, the leisured magnate in his library of rare books is a nearly extinct species. And the obligation of patronage has lagged behind the dream of creation: *Poetry* magazine, with only 11,000 subscribers, receives 90,000 submissions a year. And how many aspiring novelists support serious fiction?

Coping with the problems of the new book market will take creative thinking from publishers, librarians, authors, and readers. But it's clear by now that the book needs not last rites but fresh air and exercise.

The full text of the article appeared on princetoninfo.com, the Web site for *U.S. 1 Newspaper*, for which the article was written.

CODA

Children growing up today may not know how to write in cursive and may become so acclimated to reading from a computer screen that they will not choose to read paper books. But many of them will, in all likelihood, still be enraptured by book ownership, like their parents and favorite teachers. Somehow, when paper meets people, a very personal transaction occurs. Technology has a long way to go to replicate that experience.

What can we expect from books in the future? We will continue to hold some in our hands even as we read others electronically, essentially sharing them with the world. Paper books are about physically retaining what is valuable, and e-books are about distributing what we choose to share. The medium changes how people treat content, but the book as an intellectual concept remains sound and solid. Electronic books will be more complement than competition to physical books, at least until e-readers solve the problem of not sounding, smelling, or feeling as nice as even the most modestly spec'd paper book.

One of the finest comprehensive analyses we found online was "The Battle to Define the Future of the Book in the Modern World" by Clifford Lynch, in the online peer-reviewed journal *First Monday* (firstmonday.org/issues/issue6_6/lynch). Here's an apt summary of the importance to consumers of e-readers (which he calls *appliance readers*), and the still-viable role for traditional book format:

Are we looking forward to the new digital genres, or backwards towards digitized printed pages as we think about digital books? I believe the current appliance readers look backward—but this is not as limiting as it sounds. There is a tremendous wealth of printed books that have already been written, and the vast majority of these can only be translated into the digital environment, not reconceptualized and rewritten for it. There are many genres and styles of discourse that are well suited to the printed book and this will not change. We will continue to produce printed books, and will transport these into the digital realm as well as having them in print. We may well see a market that embraces e-book readers for older materials transported into the digital environment and new works of authorship that wish to remain within the old genres, and also general purpose computers for access to works that are authored within the emerging inherently digital genres....

The new digital genres require rethinking and relearning the craft of authorship, and there are still many stories best told through the traditional linear book and many arguments best presented as lengthy textual passages.

A *coda* is a passage at the end of a piece—written, musical, or dance—that brings it to a formal close. In music, this part was originally added to the last movement "to clinch matters rather than to develop the music further. But in the symphonies of composers like Mozart, Haydn, and Beethoven, the coda came to have integral formal significance, becoming at times a secondary development section and sometimes containing new material. Later composers have increased and extended this tendency" (from classicalarchives.com/dict/coda.html). So the coda echoes what has come before, adds to it, and suggests new directions: the ending as a new beginning.

On that note, in today's reader-generated, reader-driven, reader-centric content-creation environment, we'd be crazy not to want to hear back from the readers of this book. And so (cue coda!) the editors and authors of this book invite you to come by eeicom.com/press/istyle, the companion site to this book, to pick up where this books leaves off. On this site, we hope to build a community of i-style enthusiasts, hobbyists, hipshooters, and consensus-seekers. Consider it your own personal microsite on quality control issues.

The editors will continue to research, update, and add to the topics touched on here, providing fresh content anchored by a lively blog. Look for analytical articles from our subscription newsletter, *The Editorial Eye*, light-hearted essays on surviving the new publishing challenges, a regularly updated list of new terms and evolving usage, a clearinghouse of fascinating and useful Web resources, interactive self-tests on the basics of editorial style, grammar, and usage—and the proverbial more.

All of us who put this book together want to help our colleagues see how the nexus of technology and information-seeking is really just the intelligent leveraging of the historically passively rewarding reading experience to achieve an interactive and potentially more valuable type of customized access to more kinds of information.

Or, as Groucho Marx said simply, "Outside of a dog, a book is a man's best friend. Inside of a dog, it's too dark to read."

Inside the dog-eat-dog world of media convergence and overnight digital innovations, we hope to become your ally in achieving what used to be called "a good read." Nowadays that also means "sticky Web content" as often as it does "so good you can't put it down," but the underlying commitment to the audience is the same. We'll talk to you more about all of this interesting stuff later and, we hope, will hear from you, too.

Appendix: Resources for Continuing Education

This list of resources is necessarily even more selective than it was in the first edition, partly because there's so much information available now on the Web itself. We've updated the resources that have held up well since 2000 and added new ones worth familiarizing yourself with.

We'd all do well to keep up with the ongoing research, scholarship, and reporting on three of this book's core topics: new reader expectations, effective and accessible information design, and the future of books.

So contributors Jessica deGraffenreid (chapter 3), Roy Jacobsen (chapter 6), and Mary Fumento (chapter 11) have listed the sources they used in their discussions, for you to pursue in more depth.

Then, to help you keep up with changing usage, tech terms, and computing style conventions, we've updated the listings of online resources for editing; glossaries, thesauruses, and acronyms; and tech terms and style.

In the information-sharing age, there's only one way to learn enough. Keep sifting critically through what's out there, but occasionally read an article, blog posting, or book excerpt that seems irrelevant to the publishing work you're doing today. The odds are good it'll be germane and even come in handy sooner than you think. And when you've found an analysis, essay, or overview that hits home, please let others know about it. In fact, let us know about it for the companion Web site to this book by sending your favorite publishing-related resources to eye@eeicom.com.

NEW READER EXPECTATIONS

Friess, Steve. "Yo, can u plz help me write English?" *USA Today* (April 1, 2003).

Howe, N., and W. Strauss. *Millennials Go To College.* American Association of Collegiate Registrars and Admissions Officers and LifeCourse Associates (2003).

Howe, N., and W. Strauss. *Millennials Rising: The Next Great Generation.* Vintage (September 2000).

Lancaster, L., and D. Stillman. *When Generations Collide: Who They Are. Why They Clash. How to Solve the Generational Puzzle at Work.* HarperCollins Publishers (2002).

Mello, John P. Jr. "Millennials Pose Challenge for Marketers." *E-Commerce Times* (June 28, 2006). ecommercetimes.com/story/Vkg5rbmxp1YTSu/Millennials-Pose-Challenge-for-Marketers.xhtml.

Olsen, Stefanie. *The Millennials Usher in a New Era.* CNET News.com (November 18, 2005).

Raines, Claire. *Beyond Generation X: A Practical Guide for Managers.* Crisp Publications (1997).

Raines, Claire. *Connecting Generations: The Sourcebook for a New Workplace.* Crisp Publications (2003).

Zemke, R., Claire Raines, and B. Filipczak. *Generations at Work: Managing the Clash of Veterans, Boomers, Xers, and Nexters in Your Workplace.* American Management Association (2000).

EFFECTIVE AND ACCESSIBLE INFORMATION DESIGN

Krug, Steve. *Don't Make Me Think: A Common Sense Approach to Web Usability.* New Riders Publishing (2005).

Nielsen, Jakob. *Designing Web Usability: The Practice of Simplicity.* New Riders Publishing (1999).

Norman, Donald A. *The Design of Everyday Things.* Basic Books (2002 reprint).

Wurman, Richard Saul. *Information Anxiety 2.* Pearson Education (2000).

Web Sites to Explore

iainstitute.org. The Web site of the Information Architecture Institute, "a nonprofit volunteer organization dedicated to advancing and promoting information architecture."

understandingusa.com. The companion Web site to Richard Saul Wurman's book *Understanding USA,* understandingusa.com exemplifies many of the principles of information architecture he discusses in *Information Anxiety.*

useit.com. Jakob Nielsen's Web site features an archive of weekly "Alertbox" columns on Web usability and other resources, including in-depth research reports for purchase.

usability.gov. A collaborative repository of information on usability and user-centered design, usability.gov includes contributions from many US federal government agencies.

THE FUTURE OF BOOKS

Berinstein, Paula. "The Book as Place: The 'Networked Book' Becomes the New 'In' Destination." *Searcher Magazine* (November 2006). infotoday.com/searcher/nov06/Berinstein.shtml.

Coyle, Karen. "Mass Digitization of Books." *Journal of Academic Librarianship* 32, no. 6 (November 2006): 641–645.

Dougherty, Carter. "As Books Go Online, Publishers Run for Cover." *International Herald Tribune* (October 8, 2006). iht.com/articles/2006/10/08/business/ebooks09.php.

Ekman, Richard, "The Books Google Could Open." *Washington Post* (August 21, 2006). washingtonpost.com/wp-dyn/content/article/2006/08/21/AR2006082101149.html.

Gnatek, Tim. "Libraries Reach Out, Online." *New York Times* (December 9, 2004). nytimes.com/2004/12/09/technology/circuits/09libr.html?ex=1260248400&en=bc31f3 ce53fcf024&ei=5090&partner=rssuserland.

Huanxin, Zhao. "Restoring Books an Age-old Problem." *China Daily* (April 17, 2006). chinadaily.com.cn/home/2006-04/17/content_568936.htm.

Johnson, Bobbie. "Will We all be Switching to Ebooks?" *Guardian* (April 6, 2006). technology.guardian.co.uk/weekly/story/0,,1747329,00.html.

Kaufman, Wendy. "Using the Wiki Method to Write a Business Book." National Public Radio (November 28, 2006). npr.org/templates/story/story.php?storyId=6545252.

Kingsbury, Alex, and Lindsey Galloway. "Textbooks Enter the Digital Era: High-Tech Options can Save Money and Boost Learning." *U.S. News & World Report* (October 8, 2006). usnews.com/usnews/edu/articles/061008/16books.htm.

"Library of Congress to Digitize Brittle Books." CNN.com.

"New Idea to Cut Textbook Costs—Sell Ads." Associated Press (August 15, 2006). msnbc.msn.com/id/14362735.

Naze, Nathan. "New Ways to Browse Books." Google blog. googleblog.blogspot .com/2006/11/new-way-to-browse-books.html.

"Publishers OK Online Book Browsing." CNN.com.

Roush, Wade. "A Good Read: The New Sony Reader is the Coolest E-book Device Yet— for those who can Stomach the Price of E-content." *Technology Review* (November 08, 2006). technologyreview.com/read_article.aspx?id=17766&ch=infotech.

Rubino, Ken. "Self-Publishing: The Internet Makes It Easier to Go from Idea to Print." *Information Today* (January 15, 2006). infotoday.com/linkup/lud011506-rubino.shtml.

Rose, M. J. "Stephen King's 'Plant' Uprooted." *Wired* (November 28, 2000). wired.com/news/culture/0,1284,40356,00.html.

Meddings, Luke. "School Says Goodbye to Books." *Guardian Weekly* (July 21, 2006). http://education.guardian.co.uk/tefl/teaching/story/0,,1825847,00.html.

"Students Shirk Cursive as Keyboard Rules in Third Grade." CNN.com. cnn.com/2003/EDUCATION/06/08/cursive.keyboard.ap/index.html.

Wayner, Peter. "Real Books, Made on the Web." *New York Times* (July 20, 2006). iht.com/articles/2006/07/20/business/ptbasics20.php.

"What is HDVD." Tech-FAQ. tech-faq.com/hvd.shtml.

"Wiki and Writing Books." wearesmarter.org/Default.aspx?tabid=78.

Wilson, William L. "High Density, High Performance, Holographic Data Storage: Viable at last?" Paper presented at THIC Meeting at the Naval Surface Warfare Center (October 3, 2000). thic.org/pdf/Oct00/lucent.wwilson.pdf.

Wray, Richard, and Dan Milmo. "Publishers Unite against Google: Search Engine's Plans could Revolutionise Book Industry as much as Gutenberg Did." *Guardian* (July 6, 2006). business.guardian.co.uk/story/0,,1813439,00.html.

Wyatt, Edward. "The Bottom Line on E-Textbooks." *New York Times* (April 23, 2006). nytimes.com/2006/04/23/education/edlife/innovate.html?ex=1172811600&en= d68b2341189033b6&ei=5070.

Web Sites to Explore for More About E-Books

Google Book Search. books.google.com/googlebooks/about.html

International Children's Digital Library. icdlbooks.org

Lulu.com. Books, artwork, CDs, and other products from a million creators on what has been called the number one self-publishing Web site. The site has 500,000 weekly visitors and is distributed to 60,000 retailers, schools, and libraries.

NetLibrary.com. An e-content provider for libraries and publishers that prides itself on being "most versatile" and supporting "the most content from leading publishers, the most types of media—including eBooks and eAudiobooks—the widest audience of users, and the most types of libraries," including academic, community college, public, and others.

OpenLibrary.org. Created by the Internet Archive to demonstrate how to make important book collections from around the world accessible online in an easy-to-use interface. "If they're in the public domain, the books can be downloaded, shared and printed for free. They can also be printed for a nominal fee by a third party, who will bind and mail the book to you," according to the site. The Internet Archive offers all media: text, audio, moving images, Web content, and software for public use.

TheEuropeanLibrary.org/portal/index.htm. Searches the content of European national libraries. "Users can gain access to the catalogues and digitized objects of the national libraries who are full partners of the service. The terms for access to individual objects by members of the public [under stated terms and conditions] are in accordance with international copyright law," according to the site.

ELECTRONIC EDITING RESOURCES

American Dialect Society. americandialect.org. ADS bills itself as "the only scholarly association dedicated to the study of the English language in North America." The site features rare finds such as the American Dialect Society's official list of "words of the year, decade, century, and millennium."

A.Word.a.Day. wordsmith.org/awad. Subscribers are a community of word-lovers 600,000 strong from 200 countries. This service, which encourages more precise and adventurous word choice, has been called by the *New York Times* "the most welcomed, most enduring piece of daily mass e-mail in cyberspace."

BuzzWhack.com. Created by veteran editor and former editorial director of UPI John Walston, this site is dedicated to demystifying business, government, and tech jargon and euphemisms (people with low incomes don't go hungry, they just have Very Low Food Security). Readers are invited to nominate terms. Free Buzzword of the Day service.

The Chicago Manual of Style Online and Q&A. chicagomanualofstyle.org/ CMS_FAQ/qatopics.html. Search a topical index for answers by Chicago Press editors to readers' specific editorial questions—and pose your own. A guide to citation style is also free, but the online style guide is available only to subscribers.

TimeandDate.com. Next time you're scheduling an overseas conference call or trying to decode the time zones in a non-US-based report, remember this site. Based in Norway and run by Steffen Thorsen, timeanddate.com includes an index of time zone acronyms and abbreviations used in North America; a world clock; a personal clock customizable to show times in selected cities; an international meeting scheduler; a time zone converter; and a fixed time calculator ("If it's 3 pm in New York, what time is it in the rest of the world?"). The site also provides international dialing codes, a distance calculator, and New Year countdowns for every country.

World Wide Words. quinion.com/words. Michael Quinion's site features a British perspective on the evolving language. His Web site and free, engaging, monthly e-mail newsletter explore the quirks, curiosities, and evolution of the English language.

GLOSSARIES, THESAURUSES, AND ACRONYM LISTS

Use these sources freely but wisely. Glossaries differ not only in spelling and punctuation advice but, at times, are at odds in definitions. The consensus approach is highly recommended. When researching a word, search several of these sites and look for points of intersection.

AcronymFinder.com. By Mountain Data Systems, this is a comprehensive database of English-language acronyms (not limited to tech terms) with sophisticated search capabilities.

Babel: A Glossary of Computer Oriented Abbreviations and Acronyms (version 00A). geocities.com/ikind_babel/babel/babel.html. By Irving and Richard Kind, this site features extensive lists of technology-oriented acronyms.

CNET Glossary. coverage.cnet.com/Resources/Info/Glossary/index.html. CNET is a major Web-based source of information on computers, the Internet, and digital technologies. This is a nice, tidy glossary.

Dictionary.com. English dictionary and directory of Internet reference sites. One of the better dictionary sites on the Web, it enables word searches in references such as *Webster's Revised Unabridged Dictionary, The American Heritage Dictionary of the English Language,* Roget's Thesaurus, and Princeton University's WordNet. Another section of the site features an online translator that translates text and Web pages from English into several foreign languages.

Onelook Dictionaries. onelook.com. By Bob Ware, this site enables rapid searches of *hundreds* of online dictionaries, glossaries, and acronym lists.

SpellWeb.com by Clear Ink. This site cleverly automates a technique for looking up words on the Web that has become commonplace. It features a form for entering a word, spelled two different ways (such as *antialiasing* and *anti-aliasing*). SpellWeb submits the two different spellings to a major search engine, such as WebCrawler, and returns results on how many times each spelling of the word was used on the Web. While this technique still doesn't ensure that the word is spelled correctly, it is a reassuring populist opinion poll.

Thesaurus.com. Online version of *Roget's Thesaurus of English Words and Phrases.*

Webopedia.com. This was one of our favorites, a very detailed, extensive technical glossary, though as a generic term, webopedia ranks right up there with webrary as sadly lacking euphony.

TECH TERMS AND COMPUTING STYLE

Microsoft Manual of Style for Technical Publications, 3rd ed. Microsoft Press (2004). The newest edition of this industry bible advises on writing for a global audience and accessibility concerns, and defines new technical terms and acronyms. It also contains sections on usage, grammar, punctuation, tone, formatting, and style problems common to print documentation, online help, Web content, and other communications. A CD contains the complete e-book.

Microsoft Press Computer Dictionary, 5th ed. Microsoft Press (2002). Over 10,000 technical terms, acronyms, and concepts of home and office technology defined and illustrated.

Read Me First! A Style Guide for the Computer Industry, 2nd ed. Sun Technical Publications/Prentice Hall (2003). The update of this industry classic is a favorite of EEI Press editors because of its focus on writing and structuring content. Includes chapters on online writing style (including for an international audience), link construction, creating a technical glossary, and indexing. Also, four immensely useful appendixes on developing a publications department, checklists and forms, correct use of terms, and recommended reading.

Walker, Janice R., and Todd Taylor. *The Columbia Guide to Online Style,* 2nd ed. Columbia University Press (2006). This guide gives advice on "locating, evaluating, translating, and using the elements of citation" for citing electronic sources regardless of the specific bibliographic style you may be required to use—whether humanities or scientific style.

Index

A

Abbreviations
  for a global audience, 98
  handling, 87–91
  style guides and, 106
About Face: The Essentials of User Interface Design, 52
About.com, 30
Accessibility
  for persons with disabilities, 77–80
  structuring information for, 47–54, 56
  style guides and, 115–116
Acronyms
  for a global audience, 98
  handling, 87–90
  style guides and, 106
Acronymy, 88
Adobe, 155–157
Alertbox, 56, 66
Aliteracy, 162–163
Amazon.com, 32, 154, 160
American Foundation for the Blind, 80
American Press Institute, 31
Americans with Disabilities Act, 80
Appliance readers, 163–164

B

"The Battle to Define the Future of the Book in the Modern World," 163–164

Benkoil, Dorian, 60
Bernard, Michael L., 12
Berners-Lee, Tim, 74
Beyond Generation X: A Practical Guide for Managers, 24
Biased language, 108
Blogging. *See* Conversational media
Books
  cost of change, 158
  cultural shift, 159–161
  e-books and usability, 155–157
  future of, 153–165
  mass digitization of, 153–154
  pay-per-print, 159
  preserving, 159
  print-on-demand, 159
  quantity of, 162–163
  storage, 158–159
Browse sequences, 51–52
Business names and trademarks, 83, 84, 91–93

C

Cambridge Encyclopedia of the English Language, 59
Capitalization
  acronyms, 89–90
  brand names and trademarks, 83, 84, 91–93
  down style, 116, 127
  personal titles, 93

proper nouns, 91
style guides and, 107
CD-ROM
   as publishing medium, 162–163
Chronicle of Higher Education, 20, 22
Citations
   CD-ROM, 102
   e-mail, 101
   electronic lists and newsgroups, 102
   style guides and, 107
   Web sites, 101
Citizen journalism, 31
Clock times, 99
CNET, 22
CNN.com, 154
Community
   building through strategic
      commenting, 38–40
   conversational media and, 35–36,
      37–38, 157
   importance of listening, 41
Compounding, 95–96
Conditional text, 52
Conversational media
   community and, 35–36, 37–38, 157
   cutting through clutter, 40–41
   definition, 35–36
   deterring poor-quality comments,
      43
   getting started in, 37–38
   listening, 41
   problem solving, 44–45
   seeding high-quality conversations,
      42–43
   strategic commenting, 38–40, 157
   style tips, 36–37
   sustaining conversation, 45
Cooper, Alan, 52
Copyright, 102–103, 154, 159–160
Crawford, Colin, 30
Crystal, David, 59
Currency, 98

D
Dates, 99
Dearauthor.com, 155

December, John, 74
Digg.com, 35
Disabilities, Web accessibility for
   persons with, 77–80
Doherty, Mick, 73, 74
*Don't Make Me Think: A Common
   Sense Approach to Web Usability*,
   53
Down style, 116, 127
Dunbar, Henry, 117–122

E
e-books
   cost of change, 158
   cultural shift, 159–161
   future of, 163–165
   mass digitization of books,
      153–154
   quantity of, 162–163
   storage, 158–159
   usability, 155–157
e-mail
   citations, 101
   to commenters, 42
   obtaining e-mail addresses, 42
   as "publishing," 59–60, 77
   typos in, 59
Eason, Jordan, 33
eBay, 32, 92
Editing
   online, 13
   print-to-Web, 60–73
   user-generated content, 33–34
   Web style, 55–59, 60–61, 76
The Editorial Eye, 74, 81, 112, 164
Education
   Internet and, 13
   millennials and, 22, 23
Electronic citations, 101–102
English
   changes in, 83–85, 125–126
   editorial choices, 126–127
   morphing parts of speech, 84, 96
   new media terms, 2–9
   tech terms, 147–152
   words to keep an eye on, 128–147

"Envisioning the Whole Digital Person," 16
European Library, 154
Exner's Writing Area, 15
Eye tracking, 12–15
Eyetrack III study, 12–13, 14

F
Facebook, 23, 26, 31
Federal Rehabilitation Act, Section 508, 78–79
Findaway World, 15
Flickr, 23, 36
Follett, Jonathan, 16–17
Fonts, 12, 13, 14

G
Generational differences, 21
Global audience, 58, 97–100
Google, 40, 151, 153
Google Book Search, 154, 161
Graceful degradation concept, 16
Grammar, style guides and, 107
Guide to Web Style, 113

H
Harnad, Stevan, 12, 14
Head First series, 50
Headline style, 116
Helicopter parents, 23–24
Help systems, 51–52
Hill, Charles A., 13, 14, 15
Horton, Sarah, 55, 56
Household Education Survey, 12
Hypertext links, 13, 15, 51, 114
Hyphenation
style guides and, 106–107
trends and patterns, 95–96

I
IIL Publishing-New York, 161
Information Anxiety 2, 48
Information structures
building blocks and frameworks, 52
multiple structures, 48–49, 51–52
testing, 53–54

types of, 47–48
varying structures, 49–51
Initialisms, 87–91
inta.org, 83
Interactivity and online content, 56
Internet
access to books and, 153–154
conversational media and, 35
terminology, 2–9, 147–152
Internet Movie Database, 51
Intranetroadmap.com, 113
Intuitive Life Business blog, 42
Iraqslogger.com, 33, 34
iTunes U, 15

J
Jargon File, 59

K
King, Stephen, 159–160
Kingsolver, Barbara, 85
Krug, Steve, 53

L
Language
changes in, 83–85, 125–126
editorial choices, 126–127
morphing parts of speech, 84, 96
new media terms, 2–9
tech terms, 147–152
words to keep an eye on, 128–147
LATCH structures
combining, 48–49, 51–52
types of, 47–48
varying, 49–51
Levine, Rick, 113
"Libraries Reach Out Online," 154
LibraryThing, 160, 161
Listening *vs.* reading, 15
Literacy, 12, 13
Litte, Jane, 155
The Lost Art of Listening, 41
Lulu.com, 160
Lynch, Clifford, 163–164
Lynch, Patrick, 55, 56

M

Macros
 to check for biased language, 108
 to convert tables, 109
Marketing to millennials, 25–26
Measurements, 58
Mediabistro.com, 60
Microsoft Corp., 102, 153
Millennials
 characteristics of, 19–20
 compared with other generations,
  21
 influences, 22–24
 marketing to, 25–26
 music and, 20
 values, 20–22
 volunteerism and, 26–27
 in the workplace, 24–25
"The Millennials Usher in a New Era,"
 22
MindPowerInc.com, 25
Moore's Law, 31
Multimodality, 77–80
MySpace, 23, 31

N

National Institute for Literacy, 12
Navigation and online content, 56,
 112–115
NetLingo, 147
Newsgroups, citations, 102
NewspaperNEXT project, 31
Nichols, Michael, 41
Nielsen, Jakob, 56, 66, 76
"Nonce" terms, 127
Numbers
 for a global audience, 99
 Internet style, 96–97
 style guides and, 107

O

O'Connor, Kathy, 15
Olsen, Stefanie, 22–23
Online books. *See* e-books
Open Library, 155

O'Reilly, Tim, 8–9, 32
Organizing material
 e-mail, 59–60
 formatting text for scanning, 64–71
 highlighting, 65–66
 restructuring for the Web, 63–64
 structuring information, 47–54
 tightening verbose text, 71–73
 Web style, 55–59, 60–61, 76
 without editing, 73
Orientation and online content, 56
Outing, Steve, 12–13, 14

P

Paciello, Mike, 79
Pandora.com, 20
Parts of speech, morphing, 96
Paul Laurence Dunbar Digital
 Collection, 154
Pay-per-print, 159
Personal titles, 93
Playaway, 15
Poetry magazine, 163
Portals, 51
Poynter Institute for Media Studies,
 14, 29
Prefixes, 93–94
Preservation of books, 159
Print-on-demand, 159
Printing, designing for, 114
Proprietary style guides
 advantages of, 105–106
 characteristics of successful, 110
 components of, 106–109
 design and accessibility, 115–116
 gatekeeping, 123
 introducing, 116–122
 making editorial choices, 109–111
 organizing content, 112–115
 priorities, 110–111
 proprietary styles at work, 111–112
 updating, 122–123
 for Web sites, 123
"Publishers OK Online Book
 Browsing," 154

Punctuation
    for a global audience, 100
    style guides and, 107

Q
Quotation marks, 100

R
Raines, Claire, 24, 25
Raymond, Eric, 59
*Read Me First! A Style Guide for the
    Computer Industry*, 87
Readability
    checklist, 115
    eye tracking, 12–14
    fonts and, 12, 13, 14
    hypertext links and, 13, 15, 51, 114
    listening *vs.* reading, 15
    of online content, 56
    online *vs.* printed material, 12–15
    type size and, 12–13
    Web style, 55–59, 60–61, 76
Readers
    appliance readers, 163–164
    and conversational media, 36
    global, 58, 97–100
    millennials as, 19–27
    myths about Web readers, 73–76
    quantity of books and, 162–163
    writing for, 61–63, 76–77
Reading Is Fundamental style guide,
    117–122
*RIF Style Guide and Publication
    Manual*, 117–122
Right Conversation, 36, 45
Rojas, Peter, 60
RSS feeds, 20, 40
Ryan, Leigh, 15

S
SecondLife.com, 35
Shelfari, 160
Social networking online, 23
Software Usability Lab, 12
Spalding, Tim, 160

SPAM.com, 83
Spayde, Jon, 86
"Stalking the Vegetannual," 85
Structuring information
    building blocks and frameworks, 52
    multiple structures, 48–49, 51–52
    print-to-Web tutorial, 60–73
    restructuring for the Web, 63–64
    style guides and format, 108–109
    testing, 53–54
    tools for, 47–48
    varying structures, 49–51
    Web style, 55–59, 60–61, 76
Style guides. *See* Proprietary style
    guides
Suffixes, 94–95
Sweeney, Richard T., 22

T
Taylor, Dave, 42
Technorati, 40
Tenner, Edward, 162
Terminology
    new media terms, 2–9
    tech terms, 147–152
    words to keep an eye on, 128–147
Text messaging, 20
Time, 99
Titles
    choosing, 40–41
    designing, 115–116
    personal, 93
Trademarks, 83, 84, 91–93
Type size, 12–13

U
UNESCO Development Goals, 12
Units of measure, 100
URLs, typesetting, 97
Usage
    definition, 82
    editorial challenges, 82–87,
        125–127
    new media terms, 2–9
    style guides and, 106

tech terms, 147–152
words to keep an eye on, 128–147
Usborne, Nick, 74
Useit.com, 56
Usenet, 74
User-generated content
editing, 33–34
growth in, 31
Utility and online content, 56

V
VangoNotes, 15
Visual dictionaries, 50–51

W
Wales, Jimmy, 33
Web 2.0
characteristics of, 30–33
definition, 8–9
functional principles of, 32–33
Web Accessibility Initiative, 78
Web addresses, 97
Web Content Accessibility Guidelines,
78–79
Web sites
citations, 101
style guides for, 123

Web style, 55–59, 60–61, 76
Web Style Guide, 55, 56
WebAble, Inc., 79
Webster's Collegiate, 126
Wikipedia, 13, 31, 33–34, 51
Wikis, 20, 34, 35, 160
Windows Live Book Search, 161
Words
coining of, 83–85
to keep an eye on, 128–147
six types of new vocabulary, 84
"Words to Watch" list, 127
World Wide Web Consortium (W3C),
77–78
Writing
myths about writing for Web
readers, 73–76
reaching your audience, 61–63,
76–77
Web style, 55–59, 60–61, 76
Wurman, Richard Saul, 47–48, 49

Y
Yahoo!, 30, 92–93
Yale Style Guide, 113, 114, 115
YouTube, 23, 31, 35

EEI PRESS
A Division of EEI Communications

Extend Your Learning...

...with EEI Press textbooks and professional development guides

Don't miss out on the guidance to be found only in *The Editorial Eye*, written by the editors of EEI Press with contributions from leading thinkers and practitioners in all walks of publishing, journalism, and digital media.

The *Eye* focuses on excellence in content creation, in print and online. Professional communicators count on the *Eye* for both practical exercises and eye-opening perspective pieces. Join our community today! Here's what one reader told us:

❝ The *Eye* has been a great resource for my two lives: the professional and the fantasy. I work in fundraising; the *Eye* (especially the "Black Eye" feature) has helped me to become a much better communicator, both as a writer and an editor. As for my fantasy life as a freelance writer, the *Eye* has been an invaluable source of information about the direction of the publishing business, technology, copyright law, and more. So many important aspects of being a working writer that I need to know about but previously never considered. Thanks, *Eye!* **❞**

$179 for printed and PDF

The *Eye* is now available via PDF at no extra charge. And coming soon: the *Eye*-sponsored blog on writing, editing, usage, grammar, readability, literacy, design, and the influence of the Internet on publishing! Write eye@eeicom.com for more information.

The New York Public Library Writer's Guide to Style and Usage
written by EEI Communications staff for HarperCollins

"We've adopted this book as our in-house style guide. With its consensus approach, each of my project teams can make their own decisions."

$38.50

—*director of communications, university press*

Real-World Newsletters to Meet Your Unreal Demands
by Linda B. Jorgensen

"I have so much going on, there isn't enough time to spend on my newsletter. This book gave me a place to start and commonsense ways to make my publication better with each issue."

$34.95

—*newsletter editor, real estate management company*

Stet Again!
More Tricks of the Trade for Publications People
by the editors of EEI Press

"These articles give my adult students a taste of the real thing and introduce young students to the important issues in modern editorial work."

$17.95

—*professor, publications specialist program*

The Copyeditor's Guide to Substance & Style
Learn how to find and fix basic errors in text and graphics, in print and online
by the editors of EEI Press

"Clear, direct exposition covers not only the most common errors in structure and punctuation but also the craft of copyediting—what's expected and how it can be accomplished. The exercises are abundant, varied, and thoroughly explicated."

$29.95

—*assistant director, university first-year writing program*

Mark My Words
Instruction and Practice in Proofreading
by Peggy Smith

"Everyone was marking up copy differently in every division. Now we all know what to look for. The result is more consistent proofreading."

$35.00

—*proofreading manager, corporate external publications*

The Great Grammar Challenge
Test Yourself on Punctuation, Usage, Grammar—and More
by the editors of EEI Press

"I have enough books of rules. With this book I've found a more practical business context for applying the rules of grammar."

$24.95

—*publications coordinator, employee benefits*

Order online at eeicom.com/press or call 703-683-0683 or 800-683-8380.
Ask us about discounts available to associations ordering 20 or more copies to sell
or give to their members. Ask us about special group rates for *The Editorial Eye*.

66 Canal Center Plaza, Suite 200 • Alexandria, VA 22314-5507 • 703.683.0683 • fax 703.683.4915

Books from Allworth Press

Allworth Press is an imprint of Allworth Communications, Inc. Selected titles are listed below.

The Birds and Bees of Words: A Guide to the Most Common Errors in Usage, Spelling, and Grammar
by Mary Embree (paperback, 5½ × 8½, 208 pages, $14.95)

The Author's Toolkit: A Step-by-Step Guide to Writing and Publishing Your Book, Revised Edition
by Mary Embree (paperback, 5½ × 8½, 192 pages, $16.95)

Starting Your Career as a Freelance Writer
by Moira Anderson Allen (paperback, 6 × 9, 272 pages, $19.95)

Business and Legal Forms for Authors and Self-Publishers, Third Edition
by Tad Crawford (paperback, 8⅜ × 10⅞, 304 pages, includes CD-ROM, $29.95)

The Writer's Legal Guide: An Authors Guild Desk Reference, Third Edition
by Tad Crawford (paperback, 6 × 9, 320 pages, $19.95)

The Copyright Guide: A Friendly Handbook to Protecting and Profiting from Copyrights, Third Edition
by Lee Wilson (paperback, 6 × 9, 256 pages, $19.95)

The Writer's Guide to Queries, Pitches & Proposals
by Moira Allen (paperback, 6 × 9, 288 pages, $16.95)

The Journalist's Craft: A Guide to Writing Better Stories
by Dennis Jackson and John Sweeney (paperback, 6 × 9, 256 pages, $19.95)

Successful Syndication: A Guide for Writers and Cartoonists
by Michael Sedge (paperback, 6 × 9, 176 pages, $16.95)

The Real Business of Web Design
by John Waters (paperback, 6 × 9, 256 pages, $19.95)

Designing Effective Communications: Creating Contexts for Clarity and Meaning
edited by Jorge Frascara (paperback, 6 × 9, 304 pages, $24.95)

To request a free catalog or order books by credit card, call 1-800-491-2808. To see our complete catalog on the World Wide Web, or to order online for a 20 percent discount, you can find us at **www.allworth.com**.